THE STORY OF
Franklin D. Roosevelt

He spent hours each day in his little New Moon

THE STORY OF
Franklin D. Roosevelt

By LORENA A. HICKOK

Illustrated by LEONARD VOSBURGH

ENID LAMONTE MEADOWCROFT
Supervising Editor

PUBLISHERS Grosset & Dunlap NEW YORK

PRINTED IN THE UNITED STATES OF AMERICA

LIBRARY OF CONGRESS CATALOG CARD NO. 56-10729

The Story of Franklin D. Roosevelt

To
The two bravest people
the author ever knew
The President and his "Missis"

Foreword

I AM VERY GLAD that this short book about the life of my husband for young people has been written by my friend, Miss Lorena Hickok. It always adds to the value of a story, I think, when the author can speak from personal contacts and knowledge. Miss Hickok knew my husband for many years both in Albany and in Washington. She knew him in her capacity as a newspaper reporter and later as a worker in the Democratic National Committee. Her acquaintance with me began in her assignment to follow me around during a campaign year, but this was after she had known my husband for some time. What is more, she knew Louis Howe, and gained his friendship, which was no easy thing to do, for he believed that the standards of a newspaper woman or man must be very high, and must, as far as possible, represent the best of the profession. We became friends, and it has therefore been a pleasure for me to have her working on this particular book for young people, as I am sure she will give a truthful picture and a vivid picture which will remain in the minds of her young readers.

ELEANOR ROOSEVELT

Contents

Illustrations

ILLUSTRATIONS

THE STORY OF
Franklin D. Roosevelt

"Thank you very much, Mr. President,"
Franklin replied

CHAPTER ONE

Franklin Meets a President

IT WAS a hot, sticky summer afternoon in Washington, D. C. The year was 1887.

A tall man in gray and a small boy in Scottish kilts were shown into a parlor in a big white house on Pennsylvania Avenue.

"The President is expecting you, Mr. Roosevelt," the usher said. "I'll tell him you are here." And with a formal bow he departed.

While they waited, the boy's lively blue eyes explored the room. Everything in it was green—green walls, green curtains, green carpet on the floor, green upholstering on the chairs and sofa.

"Is everything in the President's house

green?" he asked. "Don't they have any other color, Papa?"

A smile crinkled up the corners of his father's eyes.

"This is the Green Room," he explained. "Here in the White House there is a Red Room, too, where everything is red. And a Blue Room, all done in blue. They've always been that way. It's something we call tradition."

The usher reappeared at the door.

"The President of the United States!" he announced solemnly.

A big man in a black frock coat came in.

"Jim Roosevelt! I'm glad to see you," he exclaimed, advancing with outstretched hand. "And this is your boy?"

"Yes, Mr. President," his visitor replied proudly. "This is my son Franklin."

President Grover Cleveland bent down and held out an enormous hand.

"I'm very glad to meet you, Franklin," he said.

Franklin placed his own small hand in the huge, perspiring paw, bowed politely, and replied, "Thank you very much, Mr. President."

He backed away a little and gazed up at the

towering figure. This was the biggest man he had ever seen. Not just tall, like Papa, but big all over—stomach, shoulders, neck, head. He had a big mustache, too. Not neatly trimmed sideburns like Papa's. It covered his upper lip and hung down on both sides of his mouth. The big man was smiling at him, but not with his eyes, the way Papa did.

As the two men settled down for their talk, Franklin perched himself gingerly on a chair. He remembered Mama's parting orders not to muss the pleats in his kilts.

Those hated kilts! Skirts, he called them. They were for girls. Over and over again Mama had told him that in Scotland, where some of his ancestors had lived, men wore kilts—even soldiers, some of the bravest soldiers in Queen Victoria's army. And that hot, bulky shawl draped over his left shoulder was his tartan, she said, the blue, green, crimson, and black plaid of the Murrays of Falahill.

"You ought to be proud to wear it," she told him. "You wouldn't be entitled to if you weren't descended from the Murray clan—brave men, gallant warriors."

But that didn't keep other small boys from grinning at Franklin when he passed them on the street. "If the Murrays of Falahill

[5]

want to wear dresses and shawls, I don't care," he thought, "but I don't like them."

The room was very hot, and he felt a little sleepy. Mr. President and Papa were talking "man talk," away over the head of a five-year-old. Drowsily he remembered a song his mother sometimes sang to him when she tucked him in at night. It was a fine, booming song that she called a sailors' chantey:

Down the river hauled a Yankee Clipper,
And it's blow, my bully boys, blow!
She's a Yankee mate and a Yankee skipper,
And it's blow, my bully boys, blow!

People said his tall, dark-haired mother was beautiful—"one of the five beautiful Delano sisters." But to young Franklin Delano Roosevelt it mattered much more that she was the best storyteller in the world.

Her stories were about the sea and ships and the men who sailed them. His great-great-grandfather, his great-grandfather, and his grandfather had all been sea captains.

"To go to sea is in the blood of the Delano men," his mother told him. "Great-grandfather Delano once owned a whole fleet of Clipper ships—Yankee Clippers, the fastest ships afloat those days."

[6]

On the Clipper ship *Surprise* Mama had sailed when she was a little girl, with her mother and six other young Delanos. They had sailed more than halfway round the world to Hong Kong, China, to meet her father. It had taken them four months.

"For such a long voyage we had to have plenty of food aboard," she told him. "We had a regular barnyard on deck—cows, so we could have fresh milk, chickens, turkeys, geese, pigs, and sheep."

The part of the story Franklin liked best was about celebrating the Fourth of July at

[7]

sea. The *Surprise* was properly dressed with flags, and at noon they fired a thirteen-gun salute, one gun for each of the thirteen original colonies. Mama, who was only eight at that time, had been allowed to fire one gun.

"They let a girl fire a gun!" Franklin would say, staring at her with wonder and respect.

"Some day I'll fire a gun, too," he thought, trying not to wriggle on the big green chair.

Just then a Negro servant came in with a silver tray on which were two glasses of wine and some biscuits for the men and a glass of water and a little cake with pink frosting for the little boy. Franklin took a bite of the cake. It tasted sort of old, he thought, but the frosting was good.

Listening idly to the men as they talked, he pricked up his ears when they said something about "farm prices." Prices meant nothing to a boy too young to have spending money. But Papa had a farm at Hyde Park, New York, and every morning after breakfast the two of them would go out and look things over. Sometimes there would be a calf or a new colt or some baby pigs. And Papa would talk about his horses, which were trotters that could go very fast and win races.

FRANKLIN MEETS A PRESIDENT

Franklin was going to have a dog of his very own when they got home. Uncle Warren Delano had promised it to him, a red setter puppy! Papa had said he would have to take care of it himself, but that would be fun.

He gave a little homesick sigh as he thought of the long, cool drive from the Albany Post Road back to the big old house at Hyde Park. First, of course, they would have to take a long train ride from Washington to New York. Then there would be another train ride to a place called Poughkeepsie.

It might even be night when they reached the big house with its shady verandas looking out over the wide Hudson River valley. But whenever it was, Franklin decided, he would go straight up to the tower room, which was his playroom, and make sure that his seaman's chest, which Grandfather Delano had given him, was still there. A genuine seaman's chest, worn and battered by many voyages, it was his most prized possession.

The two men stood up, and Franklin slid off his chair. The President shook hands with his father, then turned and placed his big hand on the boy's blond head.

"Franklin," he said in a deep, rumbling voice, "I give you this wish to remember.

[9]

He would go straight up to the tower room

Pray God He never lets you become President of the United States."

A few moments later Franklin and his father stepped into the carriage which was waiting at the door.

As the coachman headed the horses through the big iron gates out into Pennsylvania Avenue, Franklin looked up at his father.

"Papa," he asked, "is it a bad thing to be President of the United States?"

Papa looked amused.

"Most men wouldn't think so," he said. Then in a more serious tone he added, "But it's a hard job, with many big problems and worries."

For a moment the boy's admiring gaze followed a team of huge draft horses hauling a dray loaded with big cakes of ice. Then he turned again to his father.

"Anyway, I wouldn't want to be President," he said. "I'm going to be a sailor-man!"

CHAPTER TWO

The Fox Hunt

Hutchins, the Roosevelt family coachman, watched approvingly as young Franklin swung himself lightly into the saddle and gathered up the reins.

"You keep that pony looking nice," he remarked.

A pleased smile lighted up the boy's face. "Thank you, Hutchins," he said and leaned forward to pat Debbie's glossy neck.

It made him happy to be praised by the coachman, for Hutchins knew all about horses. And ever since Franklin had found Debbie in her box stall, on his seventh birthday, he, himself, had been responsible for her care.

He had been responsible for Marksman,

[*12*]

too, right from the start. At first his mother had thought he was too young, at the age of five, to take on the care and training of a lively, inquisitive pup.

But his father had said, "He's old enough. I want him to have a pony, too, when he's a little older. But he must learn that a dog or a pony is not just another plaything to be put aside and forgotten when something else comes along. The best way for him to learn is by taking care of the animals himself."

With Marksman, it had been mostly a matter of remembering. More than once, Franklin had almost forgotten to feed his little Irish setter pup. But he usually remembered without being reminded by one of the grownups. And Marksman was now a handsome, well-mannered dog.

But taking care of Debbie was a real chore, even now when Franklin was eight and tall for his age. Not only must she be fed, watered, and exercised—she must be kept clean.

Her stall must be cleaned out every day, too, and that wasn't any picnic. The grooming was more fun. From Hutchins and from the groom in the big stables on the Rogers place, where Franklin went to play with his best friend, Edmund, he had learned how to sponge her down. He had also learned how to curry and brush her until her coat shone like brown satin, how to comb her mane and tail, and even how to polish her hoofs. He was proud of her, and now it was nice to get compliments from Hutchins.

Still smiling, the boy clucked softly to Debbie and rode out into the bright October sunshine. Marksman, who had been hanging around the stable door, all aquiver in his eagerness to be off, raced on ahead. Debbie danced a little and tossed her head, sniffing the crisp air as they followed the drive along the tall hemlock hedge.

"Where to, old girl?" Franklin murmured as they followed the long driveway down to the entrance of the Post Road.

Suddenly he stiffened in the saddle, a shiver of excitement running through him. Debbie pricked up her ears, and Marksman stopped in his tracks, his tail straight out behind him like a feathered arrow. They had heard it, too! A long, musical note on a horn, and the yelping and baying of foxhounds!

This was the morning of the hunt which had been organized by Edmund's father, Colonel Rogers. There had been a lot of talk about it, and Papa, in red coat and topper,

[*14*]

The boy rode out into the bright October sunshine

had ridden off right after breakfast to meet Colonel Rogers and the other hunters.

Franklin knew that they would ride after the hounds, which had been turned loose on the scent of a fox. The first man on the scene when they caught up with it would get its bushy tail, which they called its "brush," as a trophy.

"Come on," he cried to Debbie.

At a canter, Debbie started down the driveway. Marksman raced excitedly hither and yon. There it was again! The horn and the baying of hounds. Debbie tossed her head and pulled a little.

They were out on the Post Road, headed toward the Rogers place, when Franklin caught his first glimpse of the hunt. He did not see the fox, but out of a patch of woods came the hounds, circling about, noses to the ground, tails wagging high. Suddenly one of them streaked off across the field, the others after him, baying in ecstasy.

There was a flash of scarlet and a great pounding of hoofs. The riders were out of the woods now, racing across the field, in the direction of the Roosevelts' farm. Franklin pulled Debbie up short, turned in the saddle, and watched them go over an old stone fence, the horses flying as though they had wings. Tingling with excitement, he swung Debbie around.

"Let's go!" he sang out and dug his knees into the saddle.

Laying back her ears, Debbie leaped forward. They were off down the Post Road at a gallop. Over the fence and across the field went Marksman, like a streak of red lightning.

Franklin's problem was how to get over into those fields. Debbie couldn't jump fences. Her little legs were sturdy, but short. His only chance would be to reach a farm road that cut through the fields. It wasn't far.

"Come on, Debbie! Catch 'em!"

Faster and faster—Debbie was giving him every ounce of strength, every last measure of speed she could muster. He could feel her straining as he pressed his legs tight against her sides.

The farm road—here! It was softer, the going was heavier. Debbie was lathering up. Streaks of foam blew back against his face as he lay forward in the saddle, his cheek almost against her neck.

Then he saw something that made him

gasp in dismay. Hounds and riders had changed their course. They'd circled about, doubling back toward the Post Road. Jerking Debbie up on her haunches, he wheeled about. Back on the Post Road, he saw them far ahead, taking the last fence and racing down the highway.

They had stopped on a little knoll back of Uncle John's house when he saw them again. The horses and dogs were milling about. Once more Debbie responded, in one last desperate burst of speed. One of the riders had dismounted and was holding something high in the air, out of reach of the yelping hounds. The hunt was over.

Franklin had stopped on the edge of the crowd when he saw his father come riding toward him. Debbie, her head down, was breathing in great gasps, as though she couldn't get enough air. Franklin himself was panting, wet with perspiration.

The expression on his father's face gave him a start. He had never seen him look that way before. He seemed almost like a stranger.

"What are you doing here?" he demanded, staring coldly down at his son.

"I—I—well, I wanted to see what the hunt was like," Franklin stammered.

"Well, you've seen it. Now take that pony and go home. Walk her all the way, and when you get there—"

"Please—can't I see the brush?"

"You cannot. You *walk* that pony home, every step of the way. And when you get

there, put a sheet over her and keep her walking slowly, until she's cooled down. And don't you ever let me catch you doing a thing like this to her again. You understand?"

Sometime later, Hutchins, glancing up from some harness he was rubbing, saw a dejected boy on a panting pony come slowly past the hemlock hedge into the stable yard. Without a word, he disappeared inside for a moment and came back with a towel and sheet.

"Here—dry off her chest with this," he directed, tossing the towel to Franklin, who had climbed wearily out of the saddle. Hurriedly he unsaddled Debbie and threw the sheet over her.

"The lather—it won't come off—it's dried on," Franklin panted, rubbing hard at Debbie's chest. "I'll get a sponge—"

"No, don't wet her," Hutchins ordered. He handed Franklin the reins. "Just keep her walking until she's cooled down."

Round and round in a wide circle they walked. Franklin was so worried that he forgot how tired his own legs were. Finally Hutchins came over, rubbed the pony around her ears, and announced:

"All right—we'll put her in her stall now."

"Can't she have a drink?" Franklin asked. Debbie was still breathing hard.

"Not now," Hutchins said. "You just leave her now. I'll watch her."

All that afternoon Franklin moped about in the tower room. Even his stamp collection which he usually found so fascinating, failed to interest him. When he went down to dinner, his parents acted as though nothing had happened. Debbie was not mentioned.

"Let's go in the library and have a talk," his father said when dinner was finally over. His expression was serious, but not stern as it had been that morning. Slowly he lighted his cigar.

"I was harsh with you this morning," he said, "but it was a terrible thing you did to Debbie. You might have broken her wind, and she never would have been worth anything again."

"But, Papa," Franklin protested, "I didn't hit her or anything. She acted like she wanted to run—as if she wanted to catch up just as much as I did."

His father shook his head.

"You're her master," he said. "She'd try to do anything you expected of her—even if it killed her. A good master never asks a good

[21]

horse to do more than it can do. I think you understand now?"

Franklin nodded soberly. His father stood up.

"Now let's go out and have a look at her," he said.

Covered with a warm blanket, Debbie was lying down in her stall. She did not attempt to get up but nuzzled Franklin's hand with her velvety nose. She was not breathing hard any more. She just seemed tired, he thought. Her eyes looked dull in the lantern light. Franklin felt tight in his throat, as though he were going to cry.

As they walked back to the house in the darkness, he felt a hand on his shoulder.

"Don't worry," his father was saying gently. "You won't be able to ride her for a while. She's had a chill, and now it's turned into a cold. But she's going to be all right. I promise you that."

CHAPTER THREE

A Boy and His Gun

"Papa, I want a shotgun."

If James Roosevelt was startled at this request from his ten-year-old son, he did not show it. Quietly he asked:

"What for?"

"To shoot birds with," Franklin replied.

"But I thought you loved birds," his father protested mildly. "I shouldn't think you'd want to shoot them."

"It's to make a collection, like the one they have in the Museum of Natural History," Franklin explained. "Only this will be a collection of just the birds we have around Hyde Park."

He spoke confidently, for he felt sure that

his father would not turn him down with an unexplained, grown-up *no*. They were great friends, these two. They talked things over, man to man, and they had grand times together.

This sunny morning in May they were riding along a wooded trail together. Papa was on his big horse, Bobby, and Franklin on sturdy little Debbie.

Papa looked down at Franklin thoughtfully. The boy's mother had told him how their son had spent many hours at the museum during the weeks they had been in New York that winter. Franklin had asked so many questions of workers there that she was afraid he might be making a nuisance of himself.

"They told me the rules at the museum," Franklin was saying earnestly. "You shoot only one pair of each kind. And of course you don't shoot any at all during nesting time. And I want to learn how to mount them, too. I can get a book that tells how."

They rode along in silence for a few moments. Gently flicking a fly off Bobby's neck with his riding crop, Papa remarked:

"I should think your stamps would keep you pretty busy."

Franklin's mother had started a stamp collection years ago, when she was a little girl in China. When she grew up she had given it to her brother, who had added to it through the years and had finally handed it over to Franklin. With these and the small collection his father had helped him start when he was five, he now had about 3,000 stamps.

"Sure, they keep me pretty busy," he answered. "But stamps are for evenings and rainy days. This is going to be for outdoors." His father nodded understandingly.

"Well," his father said, "ten years old is a little young. You are a trustworthy boy, and I have a lot of confidence in you. But you could do a lot of damage with a gun. You might hurt somebody."

Franklin looked thoughtful.

"Yes, I guess so," he said with a little sigh. "But you could show me how to handle it, Papa. And I'd be very, very careful. Honest!"

"I'm sure you would," his father smiled. "Perhaps when you're a little older—"

"When I'm eleven, maybe?"

"Perhaps. I think we'd better talk it over with your mother."

They did, at dinner that night. Mama didn't say no—Franklin's parents believed in talking things over with him before giving orders—but it was apparent that the idea of his having a gun when he was so young worried her. So the subject was dropped. Franklin spent a lot of time that summer shooting at a target with a bow and arrows.

When he ran down to breakfast on the morning of his eleventh birthday, however, he found a real surprise. To his delight, there was a fine small-bore shotgun among the presents piled on a chair next to his place at the table.

[26]

Right after breakfast his father started showing him how to handle it and how to take care of it. He showed him how to break it to load it and unload it, how to clean it and oil it. He laid down some rules:

"Never put your gun away dirty. Gun powder makes metal corrode.

"Never leave it lying around loaded. Somebody might trip over it, or pick it up to look at it, not realizing it was loaded.

"Never point it at anybody—not even if you are sure it isn't loaded. Carry it over your arm, this way, with the muzzle pointed down and away from you.

"To put it on safety, you pull the hammer halfway back with your thumb, like this, and let it drop into place. See? Now if you squeeze the trigger, it can't go off. Here—you try it.

"Good! Now remember to keep it on safety until you're ready to shoot. If you forget, you may squeeze the trigger and the gun will go off when you don't expect it to. Now let's see you take aim."

After Franklin had practiced over and over again, his father finally said:

"All right—let's go out and see how good a shot you're going to be."

Franklin had a good eye and a steady hand.

[27]

He showed him how to break it to load it

He had been out only a few times when he got his first specimen. This was a big black crow, which his father sent to a taxidermist in New York to be mounted. After that Franklin's collection grew steadily.

At mounting his specimens he was not quite so successful. He hadn't much stomach for it—his mother said he turned green, as if he was going to be sick. He kept at it until he knew how to do it. But finally he agreed to turn the job over to a taxidermist, who could do it better than he.

During the first few months his father went with him on his shooting expeditions. But by the following winter he was permitted to go alone.

One April afternoon when his father was in New York, Franklin and his mother went for a walk in the woods. Franklin, as usual, was carrying his gun. Suddenly in a little pine tree ahead he saw a bird he had been trying for weeks to get for his collection, a little pine finch.

He was excited and, without thinking, he tightened his grip on the trigger as he started to raise his gun. There was a loud bang, and his mother screamed. Fortunately the shot went into the ground, and nobody was hurt.

"I guess I forgot to put the gun on safety after the last time I used it," he said miserably as he and his father sat in front of the library fire that evening. He was still a little pale.

His father studied his cigar for a moment and then asked quietly:

"What do you think we ought to do about it?"

Franklin swallowed a couple of times. Slowly he replied, "Maybe I shouldn't have my gun for a while."

"I think we'll put it away for a year," his father said after a long pause. Franklin sighed and then nodded silently.

Later his mother came into his room with some cocoa and cookies as he was about to get into bed. "You ate hardly any dinner at all, dear," she said.

Franklin winked back some tears. "Thank you, Mama," he murmured, and turned his face away so that she should not see that he had been crying.

For several weeks he missed his gun sorely. But when warm weather came, he and his parents went to their summer home on Campobello Island, off the coast of Maine. And Franklin was so busy learning to sail his

"You hardly ate any dinner at all, dear," she said

father's new schooner *Half Moon* that he seldom thought of shooting.

Not until fall did he begin to wish again for a chance to add to his bird collection. April seemed a long way off, yet his father's punishment seemed fair, and never once did he tease to have his gun returned.

Perhaps this was the reason that he found a special surprise waiting for him on January 30, which was his thirteenth birthday. Racing down to breakfast early, he saw presents piled high on a chair beside his place at the table. And propped against the chair was something else which made his eyes sparkle. With a little cry of joy, he picked up his gun and stroked it lovingly. The ban had been lifted!

CHAPTER FOUR

Every Inch a Sailor

FRANKLIN took his gun along when the family went to to Campobello the following summer. But he didn't do much shooting after all. Instead, he spent most of his time out on the water, sailing the *Half Moon*.

He was now a good enough sailor so that he could take the helm most of the time. But his father still went along, to be on hand if Franklin needed help.

The *Half Moon* was a 51-foot schooner, pretty big for a thirteen-year-old to handle. And the tides and currents in the waters around Campobello Island are tricky.

"This is the life for me!" Franklin would tell himself as the *Half Moon* skimmed gracefully along over the blue water.

He felt like singing as he looked up at her white sail billowing in the breeze.

The tangy smell in the air. Salty spray making his cheeks tingle. Sunlight dancing on the whitecaps. These were the things he loved.

More even than his gun or his pony.

Often his mother would go along on the

Half Moon. And as she watched Franklin's slender, tanned hands gripping the wheel, she would smile proudly and say, "He's a born sailor! Just like his Delano ancestors!"

Franklin knew a lot about his Delano ancestors, who had built ships, owned them, and sailed them all around the world.

Every year he was taken to a Delano family reunion at "Fairhaven." This big, rambling old house which his great-grandfather Delano had built in Massachusetts, was near a port where the whaling fleet used to come in. It was a real treasure house for a boy who loved the sea and ships.

Its walls were covered with pictures of ships which the Delanos had designed and built. Frigates for the Navy. Whaling ships. Beautiful Yankee Clippers, which they had owned and sailed themselves.

The house was filled with strange, carved furniture from faraway places. And in the attic there were binoculars, seamen's chests, navigation charts, and yellowed ship's logs!

Down at the near-by wharfs were some of the old whaling ships, with their tall masts. There they were, tied up, rubbing against the wharfs as though they were trying to get away. But they never would get away. Their day was gone. Steam engines had taken the place of sails.

Franklin would spend hours down there, visiting with old sailors who were now retired along with the ships they had sailed.

He had read a lot about whalers and other kinds of ships. Indeed, he had read every kind of book about the sea and ships that he could find.

Lately, he had become especially interested in books about the Navy. He had run across some real thrillers, written by a distant cousin who was an instructor in the U. S. Naval Academy at Annapolis.

Franklin was talking about these books

one morning as he walked along the beach with another boy, Joe Lovering, who lived at Campobello.

But the talk switched away from the Navy, when Joe picked up a stick and began twirling it, like a drum major's baton. He twirled it rapidly, tossed it high in the air and caught it, without breaking his marching stride.

"Say, that's good, Joe! Do it again," Franklin exclaimed.

"Aw, that's nothing," said Joe. "I can do better than that. Look!"

Again he tossed the stick high in the air. But this time it didn't come down where it was supposed to. Instead, it hit Franklin in the mouth.

"Gee, Franklin, I didn't mean to do that!" Joe cried, running over to him. "Does it hurt bad?"

Franklin, very pale, was holding his hand over his mouth. Joe could see a little trickle of blood running down his chin, from where his lip was cut.

Franklin shook his head. "It's all right, Joe," he managed to say. "It doesn't hurt much."

They were almost home, and it was lunch-

[*37*]

time. Still holding his hand over his mouth, Franklin waved good-by to Joe and went into the house.

But he didn't want any lunch. Although he hadn't told Joe, the pain was bad—the worst he'd ever felt. He knew a tooth must be broken off close to the gum, for he could feel it with his tongue. But every time he touched it, it hurt so that he wanted to yell!

He didn't, though, because he didn't want to upset his mother. Holding his hand over his mouth, he said nothing, and hoped the pain would go away.

But he couldn't fool his mother.

"What's the matter, dear?" she said as he sat down at the table. "Why are you holding your hand over your mouth that way? And you're pale!"

"It's nothing," Franklin said weakly, shaking his head.

"I know there's something wrong," she insisted. "Here—let me look." And she made him take his hand down.

Immediately she made arrangements to take him to Eastport, on the mainland, where there was a dentist.

Franklin gripped the arms of the chair and

never once said, "Ow!" while the dentist probed around and took out what was left of the tooth.

"Mrs. Roosevelt, your son is a very brave boy," the dentist said when he had finished. "The nerve in that tooth was dangling, all exposed!"

Franklin smiled, pleased with this praise. His mouth was still very sore when he and his mother reached home late that afternoon. But he quickly forgot it, for the mailboat had come, and there was a letter from his father, who was in New York on business. Mr. Roosevelt had written that he would be back next day and was bringing Eddie Rogers for a visit.

"Good!" exclaimed Franklin when his mother finished reading this. He liked Eddie as much as any boy he knew and started at once to plan how he and Eddie would go sailing.

The boys had some wonderful sails on the *Half Moon*. One afternoon, as they sprawled on the dock waiting for Franklin's father to go sailing with them, they began to talk about boarding school.

Their parents had decided that after one

more year, both boys were to enter Groton, a private school in Massachusetts, not far from Boston.

"I wonder what it'll be like," said Eddie. "I haven't ever been to a real school."

Franklin had. For a few weeks he had gone to a school in Germany, while he was there with his parents.

"But it was just in the daytime," he said. "I didn't stay there nights."

"Well, we had a sort of school at our house," Eddie said.

For two years Franklin had ridden his pony every week-day to the Rogers place in Hyde Park, to have lessons with Eddie and two or three other boys. At other times he had studied with a governess or a tutor. And now, when the Roosevelts returned to Hyde Park in the fall, a young man named Mr. Dumper was coming to live with them, to get Franklin ready to enter Groton.

"What are you going to do when we get through Groton, Eddie?" Franklin asked.

"Aw, I dunno," Eddie replied lazily. "I suppose I'm going to college. Probably to Yale."

He rolled over on his side and looked at Franklin.

*Franklin had lessons with Eddie and two
or three other boys*

"What about you?" he asked. "You'll probably go on some stinky old whaleboat. You're always talking about them."

Franklin shook his head.

"I've been thinking about the Navy," he said. "Maybe Papa could help me get into the Naval Academy at Annapolis."

"Have you asked him?"

"Nope. But I'm going to."

One day after Eddie had gone home, and Franklin was out on the *Half Moon* with his father, he brought up the subject. His father listened to him thoughtfully.

"Well, I think I might be able to help you get into Annapolis," he said. "But this is a pretty serious decision to make. We ought to give it some careful thought."

"I know," Franklin agreed. "But if I'm going to Annapolis, we ought to decide pretty soon."

He knew that, to get into the Naval Academy, he would first have to get an appointment, through a member of Congress. His father had some friends in Congress, but it might take time.

For several days off and on they talked about it. Papa wanted him to go to Harvard

College after he finished at Groton and then to study law.

"I don't mean you'd have to practice law if you didn't want to," he said. "I never have, although I studied law at Harvard. But it's a useful thing to know."

"Well, what could I do if I didn't want to be a lawyer?" Franklin asked.

"Oh, lots of things. You could go into business, as I did. Or—well, you might have something to do with government. You could go into politics, like Cousin Ted."

Franklin's distant cousin, Theodore Roosevelt, who lived at Oyster Bay, on Long Island, was in politics in New York. And all his relatives were interested and proud of him.

"But those things are on land," Franklin objected.

"Well, you might not like the Navy nearly so much as you think," his father said. "The Navy can be awfully dull when there isn't any war. A lot of the time you wouldn't be at sea. You'd be just sitting around in an office, doing paper work."

Franklin looked thoughtful.

"Here's another thing I thought of," his father added. "I'd like to hope there'll never be another war. But if there was, you could always get a commission in the Navy, whatever you were doing. I'm sure of that."

Franklin remained silent for a few moments. He loved his father and wanted to please him.

"All right, Pop!" he said at last, with a smile, "Harvard it'll be."

Right then Harvard seemed a long way off. Five whole years! One year, studying with Mr. Dumper. And four at Groton. Franklin had met Mr. Dumper before coming up to Campobello for the summer.

"Seems like a good sort," he said to himself.

CHAPTER FIVE
Franklin and the Polizei

Look! Cherries!"

Sitting on his bicycle, balanced against an old stone fence, Franklin reached up into some branches hanging low over his head and picked a bunch.

"Mmmm! Delicious!" he said, biting into one. "Here—have some!"

He picked another bunch, which he tossed to Mr. Dumper, who was sitting on the grass.

Mr. Dumper looked doubtful.

"Do you think we should take them?" he asked.

"Well, they're hanging out over the road," Franklin pointed out. "It isn't as though we were going into the orchard or doing any real damage."

The cherries, sun-ripened and juicy, tasted good. Since early morning, Franklin and Mr. Dumper had been on the road, and they were hot and thirsty when they had stopped in the shade to rest.

This was Franklin's last summer before going to Groton, and he and his parents were spending it abroad. It was his ninth trip to Europe. And, although he was only fourteen, already he spoke French and German very well.

With Mr. Dumper, he was taking a bicycle trip through Germany, while his parents stayed at a resort called Bad Nauheim, where they went for a few weeks almost every year.

The bicycle trip meant something special to Franklin, for he was handling all the money which was to be spent. His father thought this experience would be good for him.

"I'm not giving you very much," his father had said, "for I want you to learn the value of money. What I'm giving you will amount to about four marks a day, about a dollar. Let's see how you make out."

But to Mr. Dumper, on the side, he had said, "If he runs short, send me a wire."

So far, Franklin had done very well. "I'm

ahead of the game," he thought, popping another cherry into his mouth.

When he and Mr. Dumper had eaten all they wanted, they prepared to start out again.

Suddenly, out of nowhere, a man in a blue uniform appeared. He wore a sword strapped to his waist, and on his head a spiked helmet.

"Polizei!" he announced curtly.

And he went on barking in German. Mr. Dumper, who did not speak the language as well as Franklin did, could not understand him.

"What's he saying?" he asked uneasily.

"We're pinched for picking cherries," Franklin told him solemnly.

He turned back to the policeman, who abruptly motioned to them to walk ahead of him.

"He's taking us to court," Franklin explained as they walked along, pushing their bicycles. "I showed him the branches, out over the road. But the tree's inside the fence!"

The judge in the courtroom was not quite so ferocious as the policeman, but it was *"verboten,"* he said, to pick cherries when a tree was inside a fence. He fined them five marks—more than a whole day's allowance.

"We'll have to get along on black bread and cheese for supper tonight," Franklin announced glumly as they rode away. "And we'd better hustle if we're going to get to Strasbourg by three o'clock."

They were planning to spend the night in Strasbourg, which is an old, walled city, and they wanted to get there in time to look around before dark. Pedaling hard, they sped along the winding country road.

Presently Franklin let out a joyful whoop.

"A hill!" he cried. "A nice, long hill! Here's where we coast and rest our legs!"

They began to coast, faster and faster. As they rounded a curve, Franklin yelled, "Look out!"

Six big, fat geese were waddling across the road. In an instant Franklin had passed them safely. But Mr. Dumper was not so lucky. The biggest, fattest goose of the lot stopped right in his way. Over went his bicycle and he landed sitting up, right on top of the goose.

Franklin could hardly keep from laughing as he jumped off his bicycle.

"Are you hurt?" he asked, as he helped Mr. Dumper up.

"No," said Mr. Dumper, "but I guess the goose is!"

And he was right. The goose was quite dead!

Neither Franklin nor Mr. Dumper was surprised when another policeman appeared. But this policeman wasn't alone. He was accompanied by an extremely angry farmer.

Mr. Dumper didn't even try to understand what the two Germans were saying. He just stood watching, as Franklin politely and patiently explained what had happened.

"Another fine!" Mr. Dumper said to himself as they followed the policeman and the farmer to court. "I'll have to wire Franklin's father for money tonight."

But there wasn't any fine after all! While Franklin was talking the judge's face suddenly broke into a grin. Even the farmer didn't look quite so angry. The judge dismissed them.

"What in the world did you say to him?" Mr. Dumper asked when they were back on their bicycles once more.

"I told him," Franklin said triumphantly, "that, after all, the goose would still be good for eating!"

It was growing late and they knew that they could not hope to get to Strasbourg by midafternoon. Mr. Dumper thought it would be a good idea to take a train. They found a railroad station and started through it, wheeling their bicycles.

There was a shrill whistle, followed by a command to "Halt." Another policeman!

"Migosh, they grow 'em on every bush!" Franklin exclaimed in awe.

"What's the matter now?" Mr. Dumper asked wearily, after Franklin had spoken with the policeman.

"Seems it's *verboten* to take our bikes into a railroad station," Franklin explained. "Come on."

So they were taken before another judge. There was another lecture. But no fine. It was getting dark when they finally pedaled wearily into the walled city of Strasbourg.

They had gone only a couple of blocks when they were halted again. This time by soldiers—a whole squad of them, with bayonets on their rifles. With a groan, Mr. Dumper sat down on the curbstone, while Franklin, in a tired voice, asked what was wrong. He got no answer. The soldiers prodded Mr. Dumper to his feet and marched them off to the guardhouse.

The officer of the day was a young man about Mr. Dumper's age. He listened gravely while the sergeant read off the charge: "Entering a fortified city of the Empire on or with a wheeled vehicle after nightfall." Then he turned to Franklin with a smile.

"You don't look to me as though you in-

[51]

*They pedaled wearily into the walled city
of Strasbourg*

tended any harm to my country," he said. "But you do look worn out. I'm sorry that I must ask you to go back about a mile outside the city and take a train in."

"But we tried to take a train," Franklin protested, "and they arrested us for taking our bicycles into the station!"

The young officer smiled again and shook his head. "Bicycles on a train, yes. Bicycles in a station, no!" And they all laughed.

They finally got back into Strasbourg by train without being arrested. And after a good night's sleep, they were on their way again.

When the trip was over, and they met Franklin's parents, they told them all about the day when they were arrested four times.

Franklin's father was amused, although his mother thought it was horrid of the police to keep arresting them that way.

"Four arrests in one day!" his father said with a chuckle. "You must have set a record."

"But look, Papa," Franklin said, emptying his pocket. "One whole mark left!"

The Roosevelts and Mr. Dumper sailed for home in late August, and in New York, Franklin said good-by to his tutor. Then he and his parents took the train to Hyde Park.

A few days later they took another train. This time to Boston and out to Groton, where Franklin was to go to school.

A very tired boy walked back to the dormitory alone that night, after saying good-by to his father and mother. He was tired. But not homesick.

It had been a most exciting day. So many boys—boys everywhere. More boys than he had ever seen together before. Boys laughing, talking, walking around together.

"I'm going to love it here," he said to himself as he undressed in his tiny cubicle of a room. "I can have so many friends!"

But before he climbed into bed, he made a discovery that bothered him a little. When he went to close the door, there wasn't any door! Just a curtain!

"I guess that's so they can look in on us whenever they want to," he told himself.

But at home, he had always been allowed to close his door!

CHAPTER SIX
Boarding School Days

FRANKLIN sat alone on a grassy bank, staring out at the playing field, where the Groton football team was engaged in scrimmage with the scrubs. The big game with St. Mark's was just a week away.

He was in football gear. "Maybe today I'll get a chance," he had told himself as he pulled on his jersey before leaving the locker room.

But it wasn't any use. He knew he wouldn't be called.

"You've got height, and you can run," the coach had told him a year ago, when Franklin was a new boy at the school. "But you're too light. Maybe in another year, when you've filled out a bit."

So Franklin had been given a place that first year, not on the scrub team, nor even on the third team. But away down at the bottom, on the fourth team.

"And here I am, still down there at the bottom, in my second year at Groton," he told himself bitterly. "If the fourth team ever gets a workout at all, it's with the third team!"

More than he had ever wanted anything in his life before, Franklin wanted to be out there on the field that hazy October afternoon.

The very sounds—it hurt him to listen. The coach's whistle, his sharp commands. The quarterbacks calling signals. The scuffing and thumping as the lines charged against each other.

"If only they'd just give me a chance, so I could get more practice," he sighed. "I know I could make it. I *know* I could!"

It wasn't that he hadn't tried! Gingerly he ran his finger across his bruised and swollen nose. He'd got that in his last scrimmage— against the third team, of course.

"But a banged-up nose wouldn't matter," he thought, "if I could just make the team."

It was the same with baseball. He wrote a funny letter home about belonging to the BBBBs—the Bum BaseBall Boys.

"It's made up of the worst players in

school," he explained. But even though he tried to make it seem funny to his parents, it wasn't funny to him.

He had tried out for crew, too. But he was too big to be a coxswain and not husky enough to pull an oar.

He picked a blade of grass and sat chewing on it, as he said to himself, "There are things I can do. I am a pretty good shot. I can ride. I can sail a boat. And I can play tennis.

"But they just don't count. You've got to play football or baseball or row on the crew. And I'm just not getting anywhere with any of them."

He had a special reason for wanting to be a star athlete. For he wasn't popular at Groton, and he knew it.

"If I could be a football star, I bet they'd take me into the crowd," he thought. "Or if I was good at baseball or crew."

It wasn't that the boys knocked him around, or treated him badly. They just let him alone.

"Hello, Roosevelt," they'd say carelessly when he went up to join a group. And then they'd go right on talking as if he wasn't there!

They'd laugh over jokes he knew nothing

about. And they'd walk away together, not caring whether he tagged along or not! Whenever they did pay any attention to him, they teased him.

"You don't talk like an American," they told him. But they didn't explain what they meant.

That had happened after French class one day, when the teacher had complimented Franklin on his pronunciation of French words.

"But that's the way they *should* be pronounced," he told himself now. "Of course I know more French than they do—I've been to France so many times. And I'd be awfully glad to help them with their French. But I guess they wouldn't like it."

Once he had thought he saw them mimicking the way he bowed when he said good night after evening chapel to Mrs. Peabody, wife of the headmaster.

Franklin had never said anything about the incident, but from then on he tried to remember not to bow, just to bob his head, the way the other boys did.

"Those aren't big things, though—not big enough to make people not like you," he was

[*58*]

saying to himself, when he saw the coach beckoning to someone.

He jumped to his feet and then sat down quickly, red-faced with embarrassment. The coach wasn't calling him, but someone else.

"I hope they didn't see me jump up," he thought miserably.

He took off his football helmet and laid it on the grass. Pulling his knees up under his chin, he sat thinking, wondering what to do.

"If I'm no good at football or baseball, or if I can't row on the crew, there must be *something* I could do," he told himself. "Maybe if I got some black marks for disobeying they'd like me better."

He thought of all the times that boys had been given black marks in study hall, and how other boys would crowd around them afterward, laughing and slapping them on the back. It seemed odd to him that anyone should be made a hero for disobeying.

He didn't disobey his parents, because he had no temptation to do so. They always explained things to him, so that he knew they were right. He knew, too, that they would feel bad if his report card showed anything but a perfect record for obedience.

"But if it takes black marks to make those fellows like you—" he thought. "Well—I might go for some. Just one or two."

Scrimmage was over. The teams were running off the field. Franklin stood up, shook himself and trotted off to the gym.

"But how'll I go about it?" he was saying to himself.

The master in charge of the study room next day looked up in surprise and frowned. Somebody was singing softly "Yankee Doodle" through his nose.

Staring grimly out over the heads bowed low above their books, he spotted several of the boys snickering.

In their center, looking innocent as an angel, was a boy who had never given him any trouble before.

"Roosevelt," he said sternly. Franklin rose to his feet.

"Come here," the master said. And Franklin, with the whole room watching, walked up to his desk.

"Was that you?" the master asked.

"Yes, sir."

"Why did you do it?"

Franklin, who had talked two German police-court judges out of giving him fines, had no answer. He felt foolish, and his face was red.

"This isn't like you, Roosevelt," the master said. "I'll have to give you a black mark."

"Yes, sir."

"You may go back to your seat."

And as Franklin walked back down the aisle, he thought he saw some approving grins!

As it turned out, getting black marks didn't make him the most popular boy in school. But he did begin to make a few friends. His best friend was a boy named Jake Brown.

But even though he had found a real friend, Franklin was happy when the Christmas vacation rolled around.

During that vacation he was invited to a dance given by Corinne Robinson, Cousin Theodore Roosevelt's sister.

It was a beautiful party, with all the girls

looking lovely in their bright, gay holiday dresses. All but one.

Franklin was dancing with Cousin Ted's daughter, Alice, the most popular girl at the party, when he noticed her standing off by herself.

She was tall, probably the tallest girl in the room. But she was dressed in short skirts and long black stockings. And she wore a hair ribbon, like a child!

The thing that Franklin noticed most

"Cousin Eleanor," he said, "may I have this dance?"

about her was the expression on her face. It said:

"I want to go home! I know I look funny. Nobody would want to dance with me."

Franklin recognized her, although he had not seen her for some time. She was his fifth cousin, Eleanor Roosevelt. Her father, Elliott Roosevelt, was dead. So was her mother. And she was being brought up by her Grandmother Hall at Tivoli, near Hyde Park.

He had heard his mother talking about her, saying, "Poor Eleanor! Her grandmother is so strict with her! She dresses her like a child, although she is almost grown up."

The music stopped, and Alice's partner came to claim the next dance.

Franklin looked around and saw Eleanor still standing alone, looking as though she wanted to run away. He walked over to her.

"Cousin Eleanor," he said, bowing low, "may I have this dance?"

"Oh, yes," she said. A radiant smile lighted up her face and made it beautiful.

Franklin smiled, too. He did not tell her he'd been lonely, too, and had been left standing off by himself, at Groton. But he knew how she felt.

[65]

CHAPTER SEVEN

A Decision to Make

BUT JAKE, my father said I could always go into the Navy if there was a war!"

Franklin and his friend, Jake Brown, were talking about their secret plan to run away from Groton and join the Navy. It was late April, 1898, and the United States was at war with Spain.

Jake was all for the plan, but he felt a little uneasy about what their parents might think, especially Franklin's parents, who were in Europe.

Franklin, however, felt sure his father would back him up. Hadn't Papa told him once that in time of war he could always get a commission in the Navy?

"I guess they probably wouldn't give me a commission yet," Franklin said. "After all, I'm only sixteen even if I do know quite a lot about navigation. But we could get in, Jake, and that's what counts right now, when they need men."

Jake nodded solemnly. "Yeah, I guess that's so," he said.

"Once we're in," Franklin said, "there's nothing anybody can do about it. Sure, our folks will worry about us at first, but they'll be proud of us, too. All we have to do is to go to the recruiting office in Boston and join up."

"We'll have to get away from Groton first," Jake reminded him.

"That will be easy," Franklin said. "We'll wait till the Pieman comes on Saturday and we'll—" He put his mouth to Jake's ear and began to whisper.

Twice a week, a baker whom the boys called the Pieman drove his horse and wagon into the school grounds and sold pastries. When he arrived on Saturday, Franklin and Jake managed to be his last customers.

"Hey, listen," Franklin said to him in a low voice, "Jake and I want to get to Boston to enlist in the Navy so we can fight in the war. But first we've got to get away from here, and we can't do it unless you'll help us."

"Me?" The Pieman looked surprised.

"Yep," said Franklin. "If you'll meet us outside the school grounds on Sunday, you can hide us in your wagon and take us to the railroad station. Of course we'll pay you."

The Pieman took off his cap and scratched his head.

"Well, I don't know," he said doubtfully. "If Dr. Peabody ever found out about it, he wouldn't let me come in here no more."

"But he'd never need to hear," Franklin urged. "Nobody'll know about it except just us three. And once we're in the Navy, they'll all be proud of us. Will you take us? We'll pay you fifty cents apiece."

The Pieman laughed. "That's no money. I won't do it for a cent less than three dollars for the two of you."

Franklin turned to Jake. "That'll leave us just enough for our tickets to Boston," he said. "Shall we do it?"

Jake agreed, and arrangements were made to meet the Pieman right after breakfast on Sunday. Then the Pieman drove away.

Late that afternoon the two boys got off by themselves for a final conference. They wouldn't take any luggage, for, as Franklin pointed out, they would be given uniforms as soon as they were sworn in. He sniffled as he said it.

"What's the matter with you—you got a cold?" Jake asked him.

"I guess maybe I have—a little one," Franklin answered. "My throat's kind of sore, and I feel awfully hot."

"I feel sort of funny, too," Jake told him. "My eyes keep watering."

At dinner that night neither boy had much

[69]

appetite. One of the masters eyed them suspiciously. Early the next morning both boys were ordered to report at the infirmary. Presently one of the masters came in with the doctor.

"Either of you kids ever had measles?" the doctor asked, after he had looked at their throats and taken their temperatures. Both boys shook their heads.

"Well, you've got them now," the doctor said cheerfully.

When they were alone, Franklin and Jake looked at each other miserably.

"Of all the rotten luck!" Jake groaned. "Just now, when everything was working out right! Measles!"

"Well, let's not tell anybody what we were planning," Franklin said. "We can try it again later."

But by the time they were out of the infirmary the Pieman had changed his mind about helping them. He said he couldn't afford to take the chance.

Franklin's disappointment was forgotten, however, in his excitement over a letter from his parents. He was to have a boat of his own, one that he could handle all by himself. His father had ordered it, and it would be waiting for him at Campobello.

"She's a little beauty," Franklin told Jake. "Twenty-one-foot knockabout with a centerboard. She's got a cabin that'll sleep two. You'll have to come up to Campo."

"What you going to call her?" Jake asked.

"Well, my father's big boat is the *Half Moon*," Franklin told him. "This is a little boat, so we could call her the *New Moon*. What do you think?"

Now Franklin could hardly wait to get to Campobello. Sailing in the *Half Moon*, with his father as teacher, he had learned every current, rock, and shoal in Passamaquoddy Bay. His parents knew that he could take care of himself on the water. And he spent hours each day in his little *New Moon*.

Jake came to visit him, and they went sailing together. Then early one morning they went out on a fishing boat. They were on their way back, and the grizzled old skipper, one of Franklin's special friends, was pointing out places of interest to Jake.

"That there island off there, that's Grand Manan," he said. "You see that big pine out there on the point?"

[71]

Both boys looked.

"Well," the skipper continued, "I don't know as I ever told you about it, Franklin, but there used to be a yarn going the rounds that the old pirate, Captain Kidd, buried

some treasure on Grand Manan. It's supposed to be in a cave a hundred paces east of that there pine."

"Didn't you ever go over and look?" Franklin asked.

"Naw—I never took no stock in it," the skipper replied. "Always figured it was just a yarn."

The two boys thought it might be "just a yarn," too. But the next morning they carried a couple of spades aboard the *New Moon* and sailed to Grand Manan.

"The treasure ought to be right about here," Franklin said after they had stepped off a hundred paces east of the pine. And they started digging.

They had been at it about ten minutes when they struck an old plank. When they had scraped the dirt away, they discovered, crudely carved in the wood, the initials, "W.K!"

"W.K.! William Kidd!" Jake said excitedly. "There *must* be treasure here!"

They started digging in earnest now and kept at it all day, stopping only long enough to gulp down the sandwiches which Franklin's mother had provided for their lunch. But by sunset they had found no treasure. All that they had to show for their efforts was the old plank.

"Maybe that fisherman was playing a joke

They struck an old plank

on us," Jake said, flexing his sore muscles. "Do you think he marked that plank and buried it here?"

"Could be," Franklin answered wearily. "Anyway, I've learned one thing today."

"What's that?" Jake asked.

Franklin grinned. "Don't believe everything you hear until you've done some thinking. Then you won't waste time following false clues."

He squinted at the sky and looked out across the bay.

"We'd better get started," he said. "There's a fog rolling in."

They picked up their shovels and boarded the little sailboat. Soon they were on their way back to Campobello.

The two boys had many good times together that summer. Later they entered the same class at Harvard College, in Cambridge, Massachusetts. And there, too, they remained close friends.

CHAPTER EIGHT
Harvard Man

GOING out for football this year?" Jake called out from his room.

Franklin and Jake had just returned to Harvard, after the summer vacation, for their sophomore year. Now they were unpacking in the handsomely furnished rooms where they lived.

"Nope," Franklin replied, tossing some shirts into a drawer and slamming it shut.

"I weigh just the same as I did a year ago—146," he added as Jake came and stood in the doorway. "Not enough."

"Too bad you didn't make it last year," Jake said.

Franklin the year before had tried out for

end on the freshman squad, but had failed to make it. He was over six feet tall, tall enough to make a good end. But he didn't weigh enough.

"I guess football is a lost cause so far as I'm concerned!" he sighed.

"Well, you ought to get an A for effort," Jake said with a grin.

Though Franklin had tried hard at Groton to make the football team, he had never succeeded. And that had been a real disappointment.

But he hadn't minded so much when he failed to make the football team at Harvard. For he had found something else there that he liked and could do well.

With sixty-four other freshmen he had tried out for a place on the staff of the *Harvard Crimson,* the daily newspaper published by the students. And at the end of the year, he had been one of the few selected.

"This year," he told Jake, closing an empty suitcase and shoving it aside, "I'm going to give all my spare time to the *Crimson.* Maybe, by the time I'm a senior, I might even get to be the editor!"

Jake nodded. "Bet you make it," he said.

Franklin and Jake lived on what was

called "the Gold Coast." It was called the Gold Coast because only boys with plenty of money could afford to live there.

Most of the boys from Groton and other expensive private schools lived on the Gold Coast. And when Franklin first entered Harvard they were the only boys he knew. But they no longer seemed so important to him as they had at Groton.

For most of the students at Harvard—hundreds of them—had not gone to expensive private schools and did not live on the Gold Coast.

"Gosh, they could take things over and run them, if they'd ever get together," Franklin told Jake. "There are really just a few of us here on the Gold Coast. But they let us hold all the class offices and run everything. And, for the life of me, I don't see why."

Franklin had become interested in the students outside his own crowd partly because of his cousin Ted.

At the beginning of his freshman year, Franklin's father died. Nobody could take his place. But Franklin greatly admired Cousin Ted.

Theodore Roosevelt was now President of the United States. As President, he had a plan which was called the Square Deal.

"It means a square deal for everybody, not just the big people!" Franklin would argue with his Gold Coast friends.

Because Cousin Ted believed that everybody should have a hand in running things —not just the rich and powerful—some of the boys on the Gold Coast thought he was the enemy of everybody who had money. And Franklin, because he stuck up for Cousin Ted, would get into arguments.

"Maybe the fellows we know around here don't like him," Franklin would tell Jake, "but most of the people in this country really love him. An awful lot of people. Millions!"

Now, following Cousin Ted's example, Franklin was becoming more and more interested in the big body of students outside his own crowd.

Most of those boys lived in big dormitories around the Yard, which is what they call the campus at Harvard. The dormitories were very old, and many of them did not have fire escapes.

"Jake, that place is a regular firetrap," Franklin said one night, after visiting a boy who was in one of his classes and lived in a dormitory. "The only way the fellows could get out, if there was a fire, would be down the flimsiest wooden staircase you ever saw! Some of them keep ropes in their rooms to slide down in case of fire! Some day, Jake, if I ever get a chance, I'm going to do something about that."

In his senior year Franklin had his chance. For he became the editor of the *Crimson*.

One of the first things he did was to write some editorials about the need for fire escapes on those dormitories. In these editorials he criticized the people who ran the college for not doing anything about it. They didn't like it, of course. But before long they set workmen to building the fire escapes!

Franklin also did something about the class elections. Usually only one boy ran for each office, and he was one of the wealthy boys. Most of the others didn't even bother to vote.

Now, in his editorials, Franklin insisted that everybody, rich or poor, should have a chance to run for office and that everyone should vote. Some of his friends on the Gold Coast didn't like this. But when the senior class elected its officers there were at least two candidates for every office. And more of the big body of students voted.

Franklin himself was elected Permanent Class Day Chairman. This meant that he would be chairman whenever the class came back to Harvard for reunions.

He was pleased. But there was something else that mattered more to him now.

For he had become engaged to Eleanor Roosevelt, his fifth cousin—the tall, shy girl he had asked to dance with him at the Christmas party while he was at Groton.

Eleanor was President Roosevelt's niece. And because she called him "Uncle Ted," Franklin did, too, from that time on.

They were married in New York a little less than a year after Franklin finished Harvard.

They had the wedding on St. Patrick's Day, because Eleanor was Uncle Ted's favorite niece and he wanted to give the bride away. It wasn't always easy for the President to leave Washington, but he was going to be in New

Uncle Ted gave the bride away

York that day anyway to review the St. Patrick's Day parade.

The wedding was held at the home of Eleanor's cousin Susie, who lived just a few doors away from Fifth Avenue, where the paraders marched. And a brass band playing "Wearin' o' the Green" almost drowned out "Here Comes the Bride!"

But that was nothing compared to the commotion caused by the arrival of the President. It started blocks before his open carriage reached the house and lasted all the while he was there.

Dozens of policemen had been assigned to hold back the crowd, but they couldn't. As a result, Franklin had a hard time getting in to his own wedding! And people who weren't invited got in, while some who were invited didn't!

After the wedding service was over, Uncle Ted kissed the bride, shook hands with Franklin, and stood in the receiving line a few minutes. Then he went into the library, where refreshments were being served.

Soon Franklin and Eleanor were standing all alone! The guests had followed Uncle Ted, and they could hear them laughing at the stories he was telling.

Franklin turned to his bride—tall, slender, beautiful as a princess in her wedding gown and veil. He smiled, and his eyes were dancing.

"I guess we might as well join the party!" he said.

"Yes, let's," said Eleanor, laughing.

CHAPTER NINE

Unexpected Victory

ELEANOR was sitting on the porch at Hyde Park, when Franklin came striding in from the stable, where he had unsaddled his horse and put him in a box stall.

He had ridden that morning to Poughkeepsie, a city a few miles from Hyde Park. Some politicians were having a meeting there, and they had asked him to come and see them.

"Guess what they wanted!" Franklin said, sitting down on the top step.

"I can't imagine what they'd want with you," Eleanor said. "What *did* they want?"

"They want me to run for State Senator," Franklin replied. And he grinned at the surprised expression on her face.

"Are you going to?" Eleanor asked. She laid aside the book she'd been reading.

"Yes, I think I'll do it," her husband said. "I think I'd like to be a State Senator. It would be interesting."

Eleanor looked a little doubtful.

"Do you think you can win?" she asked.

"That's the big question," Franklin replied soberly. "But I think it's worth trying for. Don't you?"

Eleanor nodded. "Uncle Ted has always thought you should go into politics," she said.

Franklin and Eleanor had now been married five years. They had a blond, blue-eyed little girl named Anna, and a little boy named James, after Franklin's father. They called him Jimmy.

Franklin had been studying law at Columbia University in New York when they were married, and he was now a lawyer, with an office in New York.

They had a house in New York, but they spent their week ends and most of their vacations at Hyde Park. Hyde Park was their real home.

Franklin had never really wanted to be a lawyer. He didn't like sitting at a desk in an office. He preferred to be out, traveling about, meeting people. So the idea of being in a campaign, running for office, appealed to him.

"But it will be an uphill fight—I know that," he told his wife.

The area around Hyde Park, where he would be campaigning, had always been strongly Republican. A Democrat was seldom elected. And Franklin was a Democrat.

Hardly anybody thought he had even a ghost of a chance. And when he announced that he was going to do his campaigning in an automobile, people laughed and said, "That'll finish him!"

Automobiles were still a novelty in country towns in those days. The farmers hated them, because they scared the horses. And most of the voters around Hyde Park were farmers.

"But I can get around faster and cover more ground in an automobile," Franklin insisted.

He didn't own an automobile. Nor did he know how to drive one. So he rented one from a man named Hawkey, who drove it.

Eleanor laughed, and Franklin's mother looked horrified when Mr. Hawkey drove it up to the house on the morning he was to take Franklin out on his first trip.

It was a touring car with no top. It was

painted bright red, and it made a terrific racket as it chugged up the drive.

Franklin laughed with Eleanor. But his mother couldn't see anything funny about it.

"The noisy, dirty old thing!" she exclaimed. "And what are you going to do when it rains?"

"Put on a raincoat, of course!" Franklin replied cheerfully.

Anna and Jimmy came running to the door and begged to go along, but he told them no. He'd give them a ride later, he promised. Kissing Eleanor and his mother good-by, he climbed in beside Mr. Hawkey, and they started off, with a few sputters and bangs.

"Now we don't want to scare any horses with this thing," he said to Mr. Hawkey. "So every time we see one, let's pull over to the side and stop, until the horse gets past!"

And that is what they did. Never once during the whole campaign was any farmer angry at Franklin because the red automobile had frightened his horses.

"It's really going fine," Franklin told Eleanor at dinner one evening. "I stop wherever I can get a few farmers to listen to me. At stores, post offices, anywhere."

"But it must be hard work, stopping so many times, talking so many times," she said. She thought he looked tired, and he sounded a little hoarse.

Franklin shook his head.

"It's easier for me than it would be to try to make big speeches at meetings," he said. "I know I'm not much of a speaker yet. I'll have to learn."

All through September and October Franklin traveled around the countryside, talking to farmers. He'd talk to them about crops and prices. He'd laugh and joke with them and play with their children.

The farmers liked this tall, good-looking, friendly young man. They liked the way he stopped the automobile so it wouldn't scare their horses. He really knew a lot about farming, they thought, and the things he said made sense.

And so on Election Day in November, they voted for him, and he was elected.

Right after Christmas, Franklin and Eleanor, Anna and Jimmy, and a baby named Elliott, who had been born in September, moved into a house Franklin had rented in Albany, the state capital.

It was a big house. It had to be, because, as

*Franklin traveled around the countryside,
talking to farmers*

a State Senator's wife, Eleanor would have lots of company—tea parties, luncheons, diners. She wanted to do everything she could to help meet all the important people in Albany.

As a State Senator, Franklin didn't get along so very well with the politicians at first. He had a mind of his own, and they couldn't boss him. But before very long, some of them were saying:

"He's smart, that young Roosevelt. And if he believes in something, he'll stand up and fight for it."

Others liked his ideas. He believed in honest government and in laws that would be good for everybody. He wanted to help farmers, working people, and widows who had children to support.

"He's got the stuff that makes a leader," some of the politicians said, noting that many of the other State Senators would talk things over with him and vote the way he did.

One man especially admired young Senator Roosevelt. He was an odd-looking little man, rather like one of the seven dwarfs in *Snow White*. His name was Louis McHenry Howe, and he wrote for one of the New York newspapers.

"You see that young fellow over there?"

Howe said to his wife one Sunday morning in church, nodding in Franklin's direction. "Some day he's going to be President of the United States."

Franklin liked Louis Howe. But he didn't know he was saying things like that about him!

CHAPTER TEN

Franklin Runs the Navy

IT WAS Inauguration Day in Washington. Thousands of men, women, and children waited along Pennsylvania Avenue to see the new President ride past in his open carriage to the Capitol.

The lobby of the Willard Hotel was filled with noisy, excited people. Franklin Roosevelt made his way toward the entrance. This was a big day for him. For the new President was his friend, Woodrow Wilson. He liked and admired Wilson, and he had worked hard to help him win the election.

Now, as he pushed his way through the crowd, he felt someone grab his arm.

It was Josephus Daniels, a newspaper editor from North Carolina. Franklin had met

Mr. Daniels at the beginning of the campaign in which Mr. Wilson had been elected.

He had heard that Mr. Daniels was going to be Secretary of the Navy in President Wilson's Cabinet. So he shook him warmly by the hand.

"Congratulations, sir!" he said.

Mr. Daniels thanked him. Then he said, "I've been looking for you, Roosevelt. How would you like to work with me as Assistant Secretary of the Navy?"

Franklin's face lighted up in a big smile.

"Mr. Daniels, I'd like it better than anything in this world!" he exclaimed. "I've loved the Navy since I was a small boy!"

Then he paused and looked a little anxious.

"But how about the President?" he asked. "Would he want me?"

Mr. Daniels smiled.

"I've already talked to him," he said, "and when I mentioned you he said that was funny, because he'd already thought of you!"

And so in a few weeks the Roosevelts moved to Washington. They lived there for the next eight years. During that time two more babies arrived, Franklin, Jr., and Johnny. And Franklin and his mother had to have the house at Hyde Park, which was still their permanent home, remodeled and enlarged.

Meanwhile Franklin had moved into an office in the State, War and Navy building, next to the White House. And Louis Howe had moved into a smaller office next door, for he had come to Washington to be Franklin's assistant.

Because he had always been interested in the Navy and had read so much about it, young Mr. Roosevelt knew more about it than almost anybody else in the Government.

"We have a weak Navy for such a large country," he told Secretary Daniels. "There's a lot to be done. We need more and better ships."

Secretary Daniels sighed. "Well," he said,

"I'll have to get Congress to let us have the money to build them. And that isn't going to be easy."

Franklin nodded. "I know," he said. "The American people have never wanted a big Navy unless the country was at war. But look what's going on in Germany! The Kaiser is building up a large army there, and a navy, too. Some day he'll want to use them, and then there'll be trouble."

"Well, if a war starts in Europe the President will do all he can to keep us out of it," said Secretary Daniels. "But we certainly don't want to be unprepared. I'll talk to members of Congress and see what I can do."

In spite of his efforts, Secretary Daniels was not able to persuade Congress to put much more money into building a better Navy. So Franklin Roosevelt went ahead without it, as best he could.

First he visited Navy yards all over the country and found ways to improve them. He worked out a better way to supply ships when they were in port. He made firms which were selling shipbuilding supplies to the Government come down in their prices.

He wrote articles and made speeches telling the people that the United States must

[97]

have a bigger and stronger Navy. And it was a good thing for the country that he did so.

He had been the Assistant Secretary of the Navy for only about a year and a half, when somebody in Europe shot an Austrian grand duke. That started a quarrel between the European nations. Germany and Austria lined up on one side, and Great Britain, France, and Russia on the other. And World War I began, with the Germans marching into Belgium.

"We may have to get into this war before it's over, whether we like it or not," Roosevelt told Louis Howe one day. "Perhaps Congress will give us money *now*, for ships and men and supplies."

Congress did, and Franklin Roosevelt was soon so busy that his children complained that they hardly ever saw him any more. They saw even less of him after the night of April 6, 1917.

President Wilson had already been elected for a second term by the American people, who were grateful because he had kept them out of war. But the German Kaiser had sent submarines out into the Atlantic Ocean to sink British and French ships. They were sinking American ships, as well.

The time had come when the United

The Kaiser was sinking American ships, as well

States was forced to do something to protect American citizens. And on that night of April sixth, President Wilson rode sadly up to the Capitol to ask Congress to declare war on Germany.

Now Roosevelt had little time to spare for anything except his job. He longed to join the Navy, just as he had longed to join it when he was a boy. But President Wilson and Secretary Daniels both said no.

"We feel very strongly," Secretary Daniels told him, "that you are much more valuable where you are. We need somebody, Franklin, who knows the Navy as you do."

So Roosevelt stayed on as Assistant Secretary and missed the last chance he would ever have to be an officer in the Navy.

The war dragged on for many months. When it was over and Germany had been defeated, President Wilson went to Paris to the Peace Conference with a plan. It was called the League of Nations.

Anna, now thirteen, wanted to know about it. Her parents had been in Europe and had come back with President and Mrs. Wilson. They were at Hyde Park with the children.

"What *is* the League of Nations, Pa, and how will it work?" she asked.

[100]

"Well, the idea is that all the nations will get together and say there aren't going to be any more wars," her father told her. "If they all stand together, and some nation starts a war, they can say, 'No, you can't get away with it!' And they can stop it, just like you'd stamp out a fire before it gets started. See?"

Anna nodded and asked, "And it was President Wilson's idea?"

"Yes," her father replied. "He put it up to the rest of the nations at the Peace Conference in Paris."

"How did they take it?" Anna asked.

"They'll go along with it," her father replied. But he added, with a sigh, "The question is—will we?"

"Why wouldn't we?" Anna asked.

"Well, we feel so safe, with the Atlantic Ocean on one side of us and the Pacific on the other. It's hard to make the American people believe we'd probably get involved in another world war if there was one."

"You believe in the League, don't you?" Anna asked.

"With all my heart," her father replied. "And I'll fight for it, too, if I ever get a chance."

He had his chance before very long. President Wilson had worn himself out traveling over the country, trying to make the American people understand why there should be a League of Nations. He became very ill. When the Democrats met to choose their next candidate for President, they chose Governor Cox of Ohio.

They chose a candidate for vice president, too. Franklin Roosevelt!

There was a big party at Hyde Park to celebrate. Though people might not agree with Roosevelt about the League of Nations, they were proud that somebody from Hyde Park was running for vice president.

"But I haven't been elected yet," Franklin remarked to Eleanor with a smile after the crowd had left. "I think you and I are going to have to do a lot of traveling, all over the country, to persuade people to vote for Cox and me—and the League."

And that is what they did. They traveled thousands of miles and Franklin Roosevelt made so many speeches that he lost track of the number. Louis Howe went with them.

"They like you, Franklin," he said, "but they aren't for the League."

"Then I must try harder to make them understand how important it is," Franklin said.

There was a big party at Hyde Park to celebrate

Others tried to persuade him not to talk about the League.

"You'll never win this election if you keep talking about it," they said. "People are tired of hearing about the League. They don't want our country to join it, and they won't vote for a man who does."

"I'll talk about it just the same," Franklin declared firmly.

On election night, a special telegraph line was run into the Hyde Park house, and Franklin sat in the dining room, getting the returns as they came in over the wires.

When he finally rose stiffly from his chair, the returns were in. He knew he had been beaten.

Stretching his arms, he yawned a little. Then he looked at Eleanor with a tired smile.

"Well, anyway," he said, "we saw the country!"

Louis Howe didn't say anything aloud. But strictly to himself he said:

"He's lost this one. But some day that young man is going to be President of the United States!"

CHAPTER ELEVEN

Disaster Strikes

H EY, Pa, look! Smoke! Over there!"

Franklin Roosevelt and his children—whom he called "the chicks"—were out sailing at Campobello aboard the sloop *Vireo*.

"Pa, look!" thirteen-year-old Jimmy repeated excitedly, pointing to a thin column of smoke rising from a near-by island.

"Forest fire!" his father exclaimed.

He headed the *Vireo* toward the island, brought her up near the shore, and made her fast to a rock. Then they all jumped overboard and waded ashore in the shallow water.

Franklin whipped out his jackknife and quickly cut some evergreen branches, which he passed out to his helpers to use in beating out the flames.

He had six helpers. Anna, who was now a very attractive young lady of fifteen. Jimmy, who would soon be going back for his second year at Groton. Elliott, aged ten. Seven-year-old Franklin, whom the family called "Brother," or "Brud," for short. Johnny, the youngest, who knew about forest fires, although he was only five. And Louis Howe's little boy, Hartley, who had come up to Campobello with his mother for a visit.

It wasn't a very bad fire. Fortunately they had reached it before it got a real start. But it was late afternoon when they finally moored the *Vireo* at their own dock.

Their eyes were red and smarting from the smoke. Their clothes were full of little holes where sparks had hit them. And they looked as though they had been cleaning out a furnace.

"Who's for a swim?" Franklin called out. "Come on—I'll race you!"

With yips of joy, they ripped off the clothes they had worn over their bathing suits and started running to a lake inside the beach on the other side of Campobello Island.

Chief, Anna's big police dog, came bounding out to join the chase, barking joyfully.

Franklin's long legs were strong and swift,

and he reached the lake first, diving in without even stopping to catch his breath.

After they had finished their swim Elliott suggested, "Let's run across the beach and take a dip in the bay."

"Okay," his father agreed. "But just one."

The water in the lake was comparatively warm. But even in August the water outside was so cold that nobody could stay in longer than a few minutes.

They dog-trotted home after their dip in the bay. And as he crossed the veranda,

[*107*]

Franklin noticed a pile of letters and newspapers on a table. The mailboat had come in. He sorted out the letters addressed to him and dropped into a chair to glance through them. There was a long one from his office in New York. He would have to answer it tomorrow.

As he sat reading his mail he realized that he was very, very tired. He couldn't remember ever having felt so tired before.

The weather in New York had been sizzling hot, and he had been there until a few days ago, working long hours. For he had opened a law office and had also taken a job as vice president of a life insurance company.

"A vacation at Campobello will do me a world of good," he thought. "And tomorrow I'll go with the chicks on a camping trip. That will be a lot of fun."

He looked up as Eleanor came out on the veranda.

"Franklin, do get out of that wet bathing suit before you catch cold!" she said.

"Just a minute," he murmured and finished the letter he was reading.

His teeth were chattering when he started upstairs to dress, and he had a chill. At dinner he said he was aching all over and he guessed he was coming down with a cold. Excusing himself from the table, he went upstairs.

He was about to get into bed, when he heard Franklin, Jr., wailing in the hall downstairs. He went out and leaned over the banister and called down, "What's the matter?"

"He says if you're going to have a cold and be sick, we can't go on the camping trip," Jimmy explained.

His father's voice was strong and cheerful as he called back, "Don't worry about it, Brud! We'll go. It takes more than a cold to get your old man down!"

Next morning, however, Franklin wasn't feeling any better. But he got up, shaved, and started to dress. His left leg felt weak, he noticed, as if it was going to give way.

"Just some muscular thing," he told himself. "If I keep moving about, it will go away."

But it didn't. He still ached all over, and he felt so sick that he went back to bed. Presently his wife came in with a thermometer. He had a temperature of 102°!

Eleanor sent the children off on their camping trip with Mrs. Howe and Captain Franklin Calder, a friend of the family who lived at Campobello, in charge. Then she called the doctor. The doctor thought it probably was a very bad cold. He told him to stay in bed and said he'd be back tomorrow.

By the next morning both of Franklin Roosevelt's legs were so weak that he couldn't stand up. And by evening he couldn't move them at all. The doctor was worried.

"This isn't just a cold," he said. "It may be some nerve trouble. I think we'd better call in somebody who knows more about such things than I do."

Louis Howe had arrived that day for his vacation. He called another doctor in—a specialist who said that the patient might have a blood clot in his spinal column. If so, it would take him a long time to get over it, and he would need good nursing. His legs and feet should be massaged.

Fortunately Eleanor was an excellent nurse. She had learned about nursing from Miss Spring, the nurse who was with her when her babies were born. Now she slept on a window seat in her husband's room, so she would always be there if he needed her. And she and Louis massaged his legs and feet.

For Franklin this was sheer agony. His legs and feet were so sensitive that they hurt if anybody even touched the sheet! But he gritted his teeth and bore the pain without complaining.

He wasn't getting any better, though. His temperature stayed up. His neck began to get stiff. And there was something wrong with his hands. He couldn't hold a pen when he tried to write a check.

Eleanor was terribly worried. She telephoned her husband's uncle, Fred Delano, in New York. He talked with several specialists. From the symptoms, as he described them, they all said it sounded as though Mr. Roosevelt had poliomyelitis—infantile paralysis. There was an epidemic of it in New York that summer.

So Uncle Fred called Dr. Robert W. Lovett of Boston, who knew more about polio than anyone else in the world, and took him up to Campobello. Dr. Lovett examined the patient.

"It's infantile paralysis all right," he said when he had finished.

"But that's a baby disease," Franklin protested, almost angrily. "A grown man of thirty-nine shouldn't get it!"

"But he can," Dr. Lovett answered. "And you have."

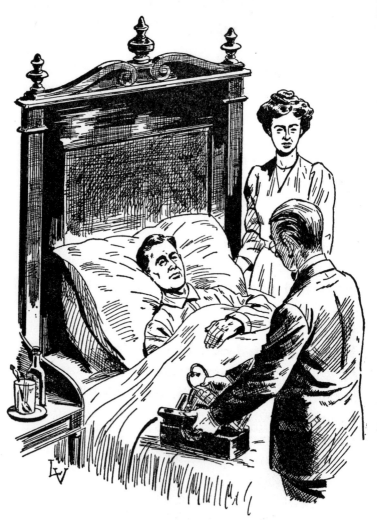

Dr. Lovett examined the patient

Thoroughly frightened, Franklin and Eleanor stared at each other.

"What about the children?" Eleanor asked.

"If they haven't shown any symptoms yet," Dr. Lovett reassured her, "they probably won't get it."

She sighed with relief. She had carefully kept the children out of the sickroom because she was afraid they would disturb the patient. Now she would be even more careful.

It was a terrible time for Franklin Roosevelt. Years later—one of the few times he ever talked about it—he told an old friend:

"Those first few days I was in utter despair. I thought God had forsaken me. But I tried to tell myself that there must be some purpose for it. Some good must come out of it. Although I couldn't see how."

Two things he knew he must do. He must keep his fears to himself and he must never give up.

"I'll lick this thing," he told himself over and over again. "I'm going to get my legs back and walk again."

He kept telling it to himself until he really believed it. And even when the pain was so bad that he didn't see how he could bear it another minute, he managed to smile and to joke.

Lying in bed staring at his feet, he would try and try to wiggle his toes. Once or twice he thought he saw the toes on his left foot move just a little.

Finally he was a little better—well enough so that he could be moved to Presbyterian Hospital, in New York. But he was still a long way from being out of the woods. Although he had got back the use of his hands and arms, the doctors were afraid the disease had affected the muscles in his back. If it had, he might never be able to sit up again.

If Franklin Roosevelt suspected this, he never admitted it—even to himself. He gloried in the fact that his arms were free. They were as strong as ever, and he decided to make them even stronger.

He had a kind of trapeze rigged up over his bed, with rings hanging down, so that he could grab hold of them and move himself about without having to call his nurse. To be able to wait on himself a little meant more to him right then than anything ever had before in his whole life!

One day his old boss in the Navy Department, Secretary Daniels, came to see him. With

an impish gleam in his eyes, Franklin beck-
oned to him to come over close to the bed.
Then he hauled off and hit him a whack in the
stomach that nearly knocked the wind out of
him.

"So you thought you were coming to see
an invalid!" he chortled in glee, as they both
laughed. "But I can still knock you out!"

He was like that with all his callers, laughing and playing jokes. They went to the hospital dreading it, thinking they were going
to feel sorry for him and have a bad time.
And they came away grinning over something
funny he had said or done.

If there was anything Franklin Roosevelt
could do to prevent it, nobody was going to
think of him as a broken-down invalid. Not
even when he was flat on his back in bed, unable even to wiggle his toes.

Anyway, he was going to get his legs back.
He was *sure* he would.

"I'll be walking out of here in a couple of
weeks," he said when he went into the hospital.

But it was six weeks before they took him
home—in a wheel chair.

When he said good-by to the internes and
nurses, he told them cheerfully, "By next

He said good-by to the internes and nurses

spring I'll be walking again. Without even a limp."

Next spring came, and one day he had a talk with Dr. Lovett.

"Do people who have this disease ever get back the use of their legs?" Franklin asked.

Dr. Lovett looked down at him thoughtfully for a moment, noting the lines that pain had drawn on his handsome face.

"A few have," he said slowly. "But it means a long, hard pull, with the most difficult system of exercises. Only in the rarest cases has the patient the energy and endurance to go through with it."

Franklin's voice was strong and cheerful as he smiled up at the doctor and said:

"All right—when do we start?"

CHAPTER TWELVE

"One of These Days I'll Walk!"

THE LONG, hard pull which Dr. Lovett had described to Franklin began soon after their talk. It started with a trip to Boston.

There he was fitted with a pair of steel braces that weighed fourteen pounds—seven pounds apiece. They ran from his hips down into his shoes. At the knees there were locks which had to be snapped into place when he stood up. If one of them ever slipped, he knew he would fall.

The braces were heavy and uncomfortable, but Franklin accepted them gratefully. For when he put them on he could stand up! True, he had to have crutches to steady himself. But he was out of his wheel chair. And that meant everything in the world to him.

There was no longer any pain in his legs. But because he couldn't use them, the muscles had begun to shrink, and his legs grew thinner and thinner.

Learning to walk with braces and crutches was not easy. Since he couldn't move his legs, he was unable to put one foot forward to take steps. Instead he had to learn to swing himself around, using the muscles in his back and hips.

At Hyde Park that summer he set a goal for himself. He would try to walk every day from the house down the long driveway to the Post Road—that same driveway down which he used to gallop on his pony when he was a boy. It was three-quarters of a mile.

Eleanor or some friend would go with him. And he would laugh and joke as if he were taking the walk for fun. But his collar and the back of his shirt would be wringing wet, and perspiration would drip down his face out of his hair. Only a few times was he able to make it all the way.

It was exhausting work. But if it meant that he would some day get back the use of his legs, he would try and try again. He didn't

He would try to walk every day to the Post Road

feel sorry for himself. This was a fight, and he was going to win it. And he did get used to the braces and learn to handle himself better. He was determined not to get out of touch with life.

It would have been easier to settle down at Hyde Park, but he and his wife went back to their New York house and continued to live there except for week ends and vacations. And he started going to his office again.

"It wasn't so hard, Eleanor," he said after the first day. "I had my lunch sent in and got along fine. You know, dear, I'm finding out that a lot of the running around I used to do wasn't necessary at all!"

Louis Howe had given up his own plans and had come to live with the Roosevelts, to be of any help he could. And with Louis to help him, Franklin continued to be interested and active in politics.

A little less than three years after he became ill, it seemed as if his old friend, Al Smith, whom he had known in the State Senate, might be the Democratic candidate for President.

The Democrats were meeting in New York to choose their candidate, and one day Al Smith came to call on him.

[121]

"Frank, will you make the speech for me at the convention?" he asked.

Franklin Roosevelt hesitated. Then he said, "Don't you think it would be better if someone else did it?"

He was thinking about what it would be like to stand up on crutches in front of all the delegates. But he didn't mention that to Al Smith. He hardly ever discussed his illness with anyone any more—not even his family. Except to say that sometime he would get rid of his crutches and braces and walk again.

"You're the one I want," Al Smith insisted. "You'd do a better job than anyone else."

So Franklin Roosevelt reluctantly agreed. Although he didn't say anything about it to anyone, the thought of standing up on a platform in the convention hall was torture to him.

"But I'm going to do it," he told himself. "I can't let this thing keep me down!"

He could feel the perspiration running down the back of his neck as he sat on the rear of the platform waiting his turn, the day he made the speech. Jimmy, a big fellow now, over six feet tall, was sitting beside him.

Finally Jimmy stood up. Leaning down, he

snapped the locks on his father's braces into place. Together they moved slowly forward. He handed his crutches to Jimmy, took a firm grip on the speakers' stand with both hands, and looked out over the huge, smoky auditorium.

For a split second the delegates stared back at him. Then they burst into wild applause. Here was one of the bravest men they had ever seen!

He wasn't the young man they had nominated for vice president four years ago. He looked bigger somehow. They couldn't see his legs behind the speakers' stand. But his shoulders had grown broader, more powerful. His face had lost its youthful look. But he was still exceedingly handsome, his smile still warm and winning.

When he began to speak, they realized even more how much he had grown. His voice sounded big, triumphant, with beautiful tones in it, like music.

The speech Franklin made that day is still regarded as one of the finest ever made at a political convention. But in spite of it, the Democrats did not choose Al Smith to be their candidate.

When the convention was over, Franklin

said, "We'll try again next time, Al. And next time we'll win!"

That summer Franklin heard about a health resort in Georgia, called Warm Springs. There was a pool there, fed by a spring that flowed out from under a mountain. And the water was warm. Franklin thought that it might be a good idea for him to go there. He talked it over with Doctor Lovett.

"It would be the best treatment in the world for you if you could stay in water and exercise your leg muscles," the doctor told him. "I'm finding that most of my patients make good progress if they can exercise in water, because it takes the weight off their legs.

"But the trouble is that water at the beaches and in lakes is too cold. They can't stay in long enough. And if you heat the water in a pool, it's like a warm bath and makes them relaxed and sleepy."

Dr. Lovett looked thoughtfully at Franklin's legs.

"You say it has helped one patient?" he asked.

"Yes" Franklin replied. "A young man. He was on crutches when he went there. Now he walks with a cane."

"Sounds interesting," the doctor remarked. "Why don't you try it?"

"I'm going to!" his patient said.

A few weeks later he arrived at Warm Springs. The place looked very discouraging. It had once been a popular resort, but now it was badly run down. "It's a wreck," Franklin reported to Eleanor on the phone that night. "But the pool—it's wonderful! I stayed in almost an hour today without getting tired!"

He went into the pool the next day and every day, until he was staying in three hours a day. The water was warm, but apparently there were minerals in it that gave him energy. And it seemed to have more lifting power than ordinary water.

So he stayed at Warm Springs six weeks. By the time he left, he could walk back and forth across the pool where the water was up to his shoulders. And for the first time in three years he could feel some life in his toes.

In six weeks he had made more progress than he had in three long years!

He went back to Warm Springs the following April, and an article about how it was helping him appeared in newspapers all over the country.

Other people who had infantile paralysis

read the article. Soon they began coming to Warm Springs, a few at a time at first. Then in droves.

There were no doctors to take care of them. And many of them didn't have enough money to get home. Someone offered to start a fund to pay their fares home.

"No," Franklin said firmly. "We can't do that. They're going to stay here. Somehow we'll find a way."

And he found a way. With his own money he bought the place and started fixing it up. Doctors and nurses were brought in. And the Georgia Warm Springs Foundation was formed. Franklin Roosevelt put $200,000 into it. It was two-thirds of all he had.

"I might never get the money back," he told his wife, "although I think I shall. If you're worried—"

"No," she said quickly. "Warm Springs has helped you so much. Others should get that help!"

By 1928, Warm Springs had become probably the most famous place in the world for treatment of infantile paralysis. And Franklin Roosevelt had thrown away his crutches!

He was now able to walk with a cane, leaning on the arm of one of his stalwart sons. More important, the doctors told him that, if he continued to spend most of his time taking his exercises in the pool at Warm Springs, he should be able in a couple of years to walk again—without his braces.

But it didn't work out that way. Because when a friend needed his help, he couldn't

*Franklin Roosevelt was elected governor
of New York*

say no. The Democrats that year had finally chosen Al Smith to be their candidate for President. But the campaign was not going well for Al. As Election Day approached, it looked as though he might not even carry his own state of New York. Not unless he had a strong and popular candidate to run on the ticket with him for governor of New York.

That man, Al Smith said, would have to be Franklin Roosevelt.

It was a terribly hard decision for Franklin to make.

"If I should be elected governor of New York," he told himself over and over, "it would mean I couldn't continue with my exercises at Warm Springs. A governor has a full-time job. I'll have to say no."

But when Al Smith called him on the phone and he heard him say, "Hello, Frank," he couldn't turn him down.

Al Smith lost the election, in spite of Roosevelt's help. But Franklin Roosevelt was elected governor of New York.

And never again did anybody hear him say:

"One of these days I'm going to get rid of these leg braces and walk again!"

CHAPTER THIRTEEN

A Narrow Escape

ALTHOUGH it was February, it was a warm, lovely evening in Miami, Florida. Thousands of people in summer clothes were waiting in the park to see the man who was soon to be the new President of the United States.

Lurking in that crowd was a crazy man with a gun. But nobody knew it yet.

In Chicago, the summer before, the Democrats had chosen Governor Franklin D. Roosevelt of New York as their candidate for President.

He had flown out to Chicago from Albany in a bumpy little airplane and had made a speech, in which he said, "I pledge you, I pledge myself, to a new deal for the American people."

Most Americans felt that they needed a new deal and that Roosevelt was the man to give it to them. So Louis Howe had been right all along. Now Franklin Roosevelt was going to be President. His plan would be called the New Deal.

He had been on a fishing trip in the Caribbean when he came to Miami that night. He looked tanned and rested when Gus Gennerich helped him off the boat and into his car. Gus had been his bodyguard while he was governor and was going with him to the White House.

The car was big and open, with the top down. Monty Snyder, his chauffeur, was at the wheel. He started the engine and they were off. Some motorcycle cops swung in ahead of them, racing their motors to let the crowd know they were coming.

When they reached the park, the car pulled up in front of a brilliantly lighted bandstand. Floodlights were turned on it so everybody could see the next President.

With his strong arms, Franklin Roosevelt hoisted himself up on the back of the seat. Somebody handed him a microphone, and he joked and laughed with the crowd, telling them about the big fish he'd had on his hook,

[131]

that got away. Then he slid back down into the seat, and Monty started the motor again.

Gus stood on the running board, and close by were half a dozen Secret Service men. Slowly the car started to move, but Mr. Roosevelt said, "Wait a minute, Monty!"

Mayor Tony Cermak of Chicago was in Miami on a vacation, and Roosevelt had spotted him coming over to speak to him. The two men shook hands.

Suddenly, there was a loud, sharp report— a revolver shot.

Gus shoved Roosevelt down in the seat and sat on him. A woman screamed. There were four more shots! One of the bullets hit the back of the car.

The President-elect was safe, but Tony Cermak was hit. Some men were trying to help him to his feet.

"The President!" he gasped. "Get him away—quick!"

But the Secret Service men had already barked an order to Monty to "Step on it!"

As the car lurched forward, Roosevelt pushed Gus away, sat up, and called out sharply, "Hold it, Monty!"

Some men had helped Mayor Cermak to his feet. He stood swaying as they held him up, a red stain spreading out over his white shirt. Somebody was yelling, "Get an ambulance!"

"Put him in here," Roosevelt directed. And he put his arm around the wounded man to hold him up.

"Back to the boat!" somebody shouted.

"No," Roosevelt said sharply. "To the hospital."

As the car moved away, he felt for Mayor Cermak's pulse.

[*133*]

"Don't move, Tony," he said gently. "The wound won't hurt so much."

At the hospital, Franklin went into an office and telephoned New York, to let Eleanor and his mother and Louis know he was all right. Then he waited until Tony Cermak was brought down from the operating room.

"We got the bullet," the surgeon said, "and we think he's going to be all right." But a few days later Tony Cermak died.

The American people thought their next President had shown courage that night in Miami. But it wasn't any more than he would need the day he rode up to the Capitol in Washington, to be sworn in. Although this was a different kind of courage.

Things had been going very badly in the United States. The trouble had started with people buying a lot of things they couldn't really afford. "Charge it," they'd say. And presently they were so far in debt that they had to stop buying so much.

Since they didn't have so much business, the stores had to cut down, and clerks lost their jobs. And when the stores had to cut down, the factories didn't get so many orders, so they, too, had to let people go. Some of them closed.

Every time anybody lost his job, that meant fewer customers in the stores, and fewer orders in the factories. Finally stores and factories were closing all over the country.

At last people grew so frightened that they began rushing into the banks and drawing out all their money. Without any money, the banks had to close—even some of the biggest of them.

That was the situation when Franklin D. Roosevelt became President.

It was cold and gray in Washington that day. A damp, chill wind blew across the steps of the Capitol where the ceremonies would be held.

Thousands of worried people stood staring up at the Capitol steps. They cheered in spite of their troubles when they saw the President-elect come out to take the oath. He moved slowly, leaning a little on Jimmy's arm. But he held his head high, and he was smiling confidently.

Chief Justice Hughes of the Supreme Court held an old Bible. Placing his left hand on it, Roosevelt raised his right hand and swore to uphold the Constitution of the United States and to perform faithfully and

[*135*]

He swore to uphold the Constitution of the United States

to the best of his ability the duties of his high office.

Then he talked to the American people.

He was deeply serious. And yet he actually sounded cheerful! It was true that we were in trouble, but we were a powerful nation. And we would get ourselves out of it. He had some ideas that would help.

Looking out into the thousands of anxious faces on the Capitol grounds, he said slowly:

"The *only* thing we have to fear is *fear itself*."

From the crowd went up a great cheer. And millions of discouraged people listening over their radios lifted their heads and drew a deep breath. They felt that they had chosen a fine, strong man to lead them.

The very first thing the new President did was to close all the banks for a few days, so that nobody could draw out any more money. When the banks were opened again, people all over the country, feeling a little ashamed of themselves, started putting their money back. The crisis was over.

A few days later Roosevelt spoke over the radio and explained why he had closed the banks. And he did it in language so simple that everyone could understand him. He spoke over the radio many times while he was President. People called these talks "Fireside Chats." Because, they said, the President made you feel as though he was sitting right there in your living room, chatting with you.

Quickly, new laws were passed by Congress to get the country back on its feet. Laws to make the banks safer, with government insurance. Laws to help business, working people, farmers.

For some of the men who had no jobs, there was a new plan, called "work relief." Sometimes the work was only raking leaves, but raking leaves and getting paid for it, the President thought, was better than just sitting and thinking about your troubles.

Some of the new laws worked well. Some didn't. But slowly things got better. And in 1936 the people voted again for Franklin Roosevelt for President.

Those were happy years for the President. His health, except for his legs, was superb. He could beat any of his sons across the White House swimming pool. Since he never talked about it and handled himself so well, people often forgot that he couldn't stand up without those steel leg braces!

When he laughed, you could hear him all over the White House. And everybody used to smile when his grandchildren, Sisty and Buzzie, would dash in to wake him up in the morning and land on his stomach with shouts of glee.

One morning Mrs. Roosevelt heard a commotion in his room. She went in and found two of their small granddaughters—one belonging to Jimmy and one to Elliott—pummeling each other on his bed. "He's *my* grandpa!" they were shouting at each other—while Grandpa desperately held onto his breakfast tray and yelled for help!

He loved to travel—on a train, slowly, so he could see the country. But he could not always go, so Mrs. Roosevelt went for him. When she came back, she told him what she had seen and heard. She went to places where they'd never seen a President's wife before—or a President.

He called her his "Missis," and often at meetings of his Cabinet, he would say, "My Missis has been there, and she tells me—"

He went to Warm Springs each Thanksgiving. Warm Springs had given him much to be thankful for. A little boy or a little girl wearing braces or sitting in a wheel chair was usually given the place of honor next to him at the table. And he would carve an enormous turkey and make jokes about who was going to get the gizzard.

As President of the United States, he decided to form a National Foundation for Infantile Paralysis. And when his birthday came around, he asked people all over the country to give money to the Foundation instead of sending presents to him.

"I'm giving the Foundation my birthday,"

he announced. So birthday parties for the Foundation were held all over the country on January 30.

Millions of dollars poured into the offices of the Foundation. Dollars to be used for buying iron lungs and braces. Dollars to pay doctors and nurses for patients who didn't have the necessary money. And dollars for research. Everyone hoped that someone could find a cure for polio; or better still, a vaccine that would keep people from getting the disease.

"Some day," the President would say cheerfully, "we'll lick this thing."

All this was started in 1938. And in New York, in 1938, a young man named Jonas Salk, who would some day help to "lick" it, was studying to be a doctor.

CHAPTER FOURTEEN

The Secret Meeting

IN THE spring of 1933, about the time Franklin Roosevelt was sworn in for his first term as President, a new man came into power in Germany.

He had a funny little mustache, and he wore a lock of hair plastered down over his forehead. His name was Adolf Hitler.

Nobody paid much attention to him at first. The American people were too busy working out their own problems with the help of their new President. And in Germany even the people who didn't like Hitler did not see how such a ridiculous little man could do much damage.

But the Germans had been having their troubles, too. Not unlike those in the United States—only worse.

So when that ridiculous little man began putting people to work building fine roads, they decided maybe he wasn't so bad after all. He did not tell them that those fine new roads were to be military highways. Before long they started calling him *"Der Führer,"* which means "The Leader."

Franklin Roosevelt and Adolf Hitler each had a dream—a plan for the future.

President Roosevelt's dream was that some day in this country every family would have plenty to eat, decent clothes, a good house to live in, and enough money to pay doctor and dentist bills, and to send the children to school.

Hitler's dream was that he would make himself master of Germany and then conquer the whole world, and become its ruler.

And so, while President Roosevelt was working out his New Deal in the United States, Hitler was building himself the most powerful army and air force in the world.

Before very long Hitler's troops were on the march. In their big tanks they rolled into Austria. Next into Czechoslovakia. And there was no one to stop them.

"But why doesn't the League of Nations do something about it?" people in this country asked.

The sad answer was that the League of Nations was too weak to stop Hitler. The countries which belonged to the League needed the help of the United States. And the United States had refused to join them.

Finally, on a September day in 1939, Hitler's warplanes roared over Poland, bombing even mothers and children as they helped harvest the crops in the fields.

The American people had barely heard that news, when over their radios came the voice of King George VI of England, telling the world that Britain was in honor bound to help Poland.

France and Belgium joined Britain. Russia took sides at first with Hitler, although later,

when Hitler attacked her, too, she went over on the other side.

All through America, people heard the news with dismay.

"It's another world war," they told each other. "It's World War II. Can we keep out of it?"

"Of course we can!" some would say. "It's not our squabble. Let them fight it out."

But in Europe the war spread like a forest fire, until it covered almost every country. And Hitler was sending his bombers over England.

In the United States, President Roosevelt worked night and day with his advisers, trying to make this country strong, in case we had to go to war.

"Make no mistake about it," he said over and over, "if Hitler conquers Britain, we're next on the list!"

So he sent guns to the British, to keep them going, while he got money from Congress to build Navy ships and airplanes, as fast as they could be turned out.

Our Army was small and more men might be needed. So he persuaded Congress to pass a law, drafting young men into the Army for training.

And while he was doing these things he was running for President, for the third time.

Some Americans didn't like the idea. For no American President had served more than two terms.

"If a man has three terms," they argued, "he's apt to want a fourth and a fifth—and to make it a lifetime job."

"But this is different," other Americans insisted. "The whole world is in a mess, everywhere except here. Roosevelt will keep us out of it if anybody can. And if he can't, he'll be the strongest, most experienced man to lead us. He's led us out of trouble before. He'll do it again."

And so, because most of the people trusted him, they voted for him. And in November, 1940, he was elected President for the third time.

The President was pleased because they trusted him so much, but he didn't feel like celebrating.

"These next four years are going to be tough," he told himself. "But I'll get through them. Thank God, I am well, although I do get tired. But when the four years are over, I hope the war will be ended, too. And I can go back to Hyde Park and rest!"

Soon after the election something happened that cheered him up, worried though he was. He was staying at Hyde Park for a few days, and one afternoon his cousin, Miss Margaret Suckley, came to see him.

She brought with her a little black, shaggy puppy, with roguish black eyes and a pink tongue.

"Would you like to have him?" she asked.

"Would I!" the President exclaimed, taking the puppy in his arms and letting it lick his chin. "I'd love it! Hey, boy—want to come and live with me at the White House?"

So before Christmas the little black dog moved into the White House—and into the hearts of all those who met him or heard about him.

The President named him "Murray the Outlaw of Falahill," after his own Scottish ancestors, for the dog was a Scottie.

"It will be Fala, for short," he said. "And

I'm going to take care of him myself, as much as I can."

So every night Fala's dinner was brought to the study, so the President could feed him. He was given a special chair in the President's bedroom to sleep in. And he went with his master almost everywhere.

Fala loved, most of all, to go to Hyde Park. For at Hyde Park he and the President could go for rides through the woods in a little car with the top down. This was a special car, with the clutch, brakes, and throttle for feeding the gas all rigged up around the wheel, so the President could drive it entirely with his hands.

"I'll tell you a secret, Fala," the President said as he and Fala were out driving one summer day in 1941. "You and I are going on a trip. Everybody thinks it's going to be a fishing trip. And they certainly will be surprised when they hear where we're really going and what we're going to do!"

A few days later they boarded the presidential yacht *Potomac* in Long Island Sound and headed up the New England coast.

"Funny time for the President to go fishing," people said. "Wonder if he'll be safe.

There are a lot of German submarines out there in the Atlantic!"

And Captain Elliott Roosevelt of the Army Air Corps and Lieutenant Franklin D. Roosevelt, Jr., of the Navy, were mystified. Both received secret orders to report for special duty aboard the Navy cruiser *Augusta*, which was to be anchored in the Atlantic, off the coast of Newfoundland.

Hardly was the President's yacht out of sight of land when up sailed the *Augusta*, bringing all the President's most important advisers. And the President of the United States was piped aboard the cruiser while a surprised crew looked on.

Several days later the *Augusta* was riding at anchor off the Newfoundland coast. The President had already had a happy reunion with his sons. Now he was out on deck. Again and again he peered anxiously through his binoculars, trying to see through the mist that shrouded the cruiser. All around the *Augusta* smaller craft moved back and forth—destroyers and motor launches. Military planes were flying overhead.

Gradually out of the gray mist a huge bulk loomed in sight. A battleship! And as she came closer, the President laid aside his binoculars.

"That's it!" he exclaimed. "Elliott, help me with my braces!"

Elliott snapped the locks into place, helped him to his feet, and they moved over to the rail. Now everybody aboard could identify the big ship—the *Prince of Wales,* one of Britain's most powerful battleships.

The band on the *Augusta* struck up "God Save the King," and as the *Prince of Wales* steamed slowly by, the strains of "The Star Spangled Banner" came floating across the water.

Standing at the rail on the British battleship, was a short, stocky figure, raising an arm in salute.

"There he is!" the President shouted. "He made it! And safely! Right through the submarines!"

Before long the short, stocky man, in a suit that looked a little like a Navy uniform, came riding across to the *Augusta* in a launch.

And he was piped aboard—Winston Churchill, Prime Minister of Britain!

Almost immediately the President and the Prime Minister sat down in the captain's cabin on the *Augusta* and went to work. For they had met to put down on paper the ideas they both believed in. Ideas for which they pledged their two nations would stand after Hitler was defeated.

President Roosevelt had expressed them in a speech a few months earlier:

"Freedom of speech, freedom of religion,

freedom from want, freedom from fear—everywhere in the world!"

The United States and Great Britain would stand for these principles, even for the smallest, weakest nations on earth. That was what

their leaders pledged. And because this promise was written aboard ship on the Atlantic Ocean, it became known as the "Atlantic Charter."

When the two great leaders had finished their work several days later, a Navy photographer came aboard to take a picture, which would be given to the newspapers to use when copies of the Atlantic Charter were printed after the President and Prime Minister Churchill had returned safely to their own countries.

Glancing about, the President saw his little black dog sitting disconsolate, off by himself.

"Why, Fala!" he called out. "Come on, boy! Get in the picture!"

So Fala bounced over on his short legs, sat down at his master's feet, and gazed proudly right into the camera.

CHAPTER FIFTEEN

"It's the Old Man Himself!"

It WAS Sunday, a mild autumn Sunday in Washington. A bluish haze lay low along the Potomac and the Virginia hills.

The date was December 7, 1941.

In the beautiful Oval Room, which was his study on the second floor of the White House, President Roosevelt was finishing his lunch. He ate at his desk. Looking out the window, he could see the Washington Monument pointing up, straight and white and clean, into the sky.

He was tired and greatly worried. Although the British were still fighting off Hitler, the Japanese were beginning to act as if they wanted to start a fight with the United States.

The Pacific fleet belonging to the United States was stationed at Pearl Harbor, the big naval base in the Hawaiian Islands. That was an exposed position.

"But if we ever pull it back to the California Coast, they will think we are weak and afraid," the President told himself.

The Japanese had sent two men to the United States to see if some agreement couldn't be worked out between the two nations. They were to meet in Washington with Secretary of State Hull that very afternoon.

For dessert, the President had been given an apple. He rubbed it in his hands and was about to take a bite when the phone on his desk rang sharply. It was Frank Knox calling, the Secretary of the Navy.

"The Japs—they're bombing Pearl Harbor!" he shouted.

As he hung up, the President glanced at the ship's clock on his mantel. It was exactly 1:47 P.M. It would be early morning in Hawaii.

He lifted the receiver and said to the operator on the White House switchboard, "Get me Secretary Hull." Then he put in calls for Secretary of War Stimson, General

Marshall, the Army Chief of Staff, and Lord Halifax, the British Ambassador.

Secretary Knox called back. He had got a phone call through to Pearl Harbor.

"It's still going on," he said. "I could hear the bombs."

The President put in a call to Prime Minister Churchill in England.

"You've heard the news, Winston?" he asked.

"Yes," the Prime Minister replied. "I want to tell you we're with you to the end. We'll declare war on Japan."

Secretary Hull phoned then. The two Japanese had been in his office when the President had called him. They were talking peace— while their airplanes were bombing Pearl Harbor. He'd thrown them out, he said, after giving them a dressing down they'd never forget!

As word went out over the radio to the American people, the President ripped off his coat and rolled up his shirtsleeves. He was not tired now. He was mad, through and through. He could have licked his weight in wildcats that afternoon.

The news kept getting worse. Five thousand men killed or wounded. Ten big battleships sunk or put out of commission. Nearly all of the 475 Army and Navy planes in the Hawaiian Islands destroyed or damaged.

All that night the lights were on in the White House, from basement to garret, while reporters hung around the entrance. Limousines and Army cars came and went. And big

crowds stood out on Pennsylvania Avenue waiting for some further word.

In the middle of it all was an energetic, strong, confident President, listening to reports, discussing plans, issuing orders.

Sometime along toward morning he got around to thinking about what he would say to Congress next day.

He would have to ask Congress to declare war on Japan, for only Congress has the power to declare war. The President cannot do so on his own.

On the ride up to the Capitol he wore his Navy cape. It was a big, loose, dark blue cape that Navy officers used to wear with their dress uniforms.

Because the President is Commander in Chief of our armed forces, he was entitled to wear it if he wanted to. And he loved it. It was loose and comfortable and did not bind his arms. Also it was the nearest he would ever come to wearing a Navy uniform, which was something he had wanted to do since he was twelve years old.

There was a roar of cheers as he faced the members of Congress. But this time he did not smile back. His expression was stern, and his voice was sharp with anger as he said:

"Yesterday, December 7, 1941—a date that will live in infamy—the United States of America was attacked by the naval and air forces of the Empire of Japan . . ."

He was hardly back at the White House before Congress had declared war on Japan. Next, Germany lined up with Japan. And we were in World War II—a war to be fought all the way around the earth.

Even while the President was making his speech in Congress, workmen had started digging up the White House Lawn. They were building a tunnel over to air-conditioned vaults deep under the Treasury Building. Here the President, his family, and the staff would be taken if the White House was ever bombed.

In the White House, heavy black curtains were hung at all the windows. A shovel and a red pail filled with sand were placed in each room. Heavy wooden crates were put over two huge mirrors in the lobby—to keep splintered glass from falling out if a bomb should hit the house.

Antiaircraft guns were set up on the White House grounds. And soldiers with machine guns were stationed on the roof of the Executive Wing, over the President's office.

No more visitors were allowed to come in and walk through the East Room and the State Dining Room. The big iron gates to the grounds were locked. After dark even the White House cars were searched before they could drive in.

But the President was too busy to be bothered by all these things. Millions of American soldiers were being trained to go out and fight on almost every continent on earth. American factories were humming, turning out guns and airplanes and ships, for Americans, for the British, and for the Russians, who were now fighting against Germany.

In the White House there were many conferences. One morning just before Christmas, after the attack on Pearl Harbor, the President said to Mrs. Roosevelt, "I hope you have no plans for this evening that you can't break."

"Why?" she asked.

"Because Winston Churchill is coming— by plane. He'll be here about six."

Prime Minister Churchill arrived soon after dark. He had come to confer with President Roosevelt on plans for winning the war. They had much to discuss, so Churchill was unable to get home for Christmas. He spent it with the Roosevelts at the White House.

On Christmas Eve he and the President went out to turn the switch that would light up the nation's Christmas tree, on the White House lawn.

The Secret Service and the Army didn't like the idea of a lighted Christmas tree on the White House lawn that year. But the President said, "Spinach! This is just about the last nation on earth where we can still have a lighted Christmas tree. We're going to have one!"

And that evening he took the time to read aloud to some of his grandchildren, and to Winston Churchill, Dickens' "Christmas Carol." He had read it every Christmas Eve to his children from the time they were old enough to understand it.

Early one cold, winter morning the American people turned on their radios to hear a familiar voice speaking in a foreign language! It was President Roosevelt, broadcasting overseas to the French people in French, telling them our troops were in North Africa!

Not very long after that, American soldiers, lined up on a North African desert, saw a jeep coming slowly along the road. On the back seat was a man in a dark blue cape, with a brown felt hat jammed low over his eyes.

Suddenly one of the soldiers stiffened, staring at the man in the jeep.

"Migosh, it's the Old Man himself!" he gulped.

Soldiers who are being reviewed are not supposed to break out in cheers. But those soldiers did, and they cheered loudly.

The President—who hated flying—had flown all the way across the Atlantic in the presidential plane, *The Sacred Cow,* to see them!

He had also come to confer with Winston Churchill. The two leaders had to decide who was going to command the Allied forces in Europe. All of the top American and British generals were at the conference. One of them was to be chosen for this important job. The decision was finally made, and General Dwight D. Eisenhower was told that he had been selected.

Before long the President was on his way back to the United States. He took many more trips in the months that followed, traveling many thousands of miles by train, plane, and ship.

Probably the most dangerous trip was on a Navy cruiser to Honolulu, to confer with General MacArthur. From there he went all the way up to the Aleutian Islands between Alaska and Siberia. The Pacific was swarming with Japanese submarines.

Fala went along on that trip. When they got back, somebody started a story that Fala had been left behind on one of the Aleutian Islands. It was reported that the Navy had had

[165]

to send a destroyer to rescue him—at tremendous cost to the taxpayers.

The President talked about this story in a speech. It was all right, he said, if people wanted to say mean things about him. He could take it.

"But Fala resents it," he said. "He hasn't been the same dog since!"

And the American people laughed with him. It was wonderful, they said, to have a President who could laugh when people said mean things about him.

But the important thing was to have a President who would lead us to victory in the war. This, they believed he would do. So they elected Franklin Roosevelt for the fourth time.

CHAPTER SIXTEEN

"Goin' Home"

THE President was happy when he woke up that April morning in his cottage at Warm Springs, Georgia. It was good to feel rested again and relaxed.

His last trip had been the hardest one he had ever taken. He had gone to meet with Prime Minister Churchill and Joseph Stalin, the Russian Communist dictator, at Yalta, in the southern part of Russia.

When he came back from Yalta the President was more tired than he had ever been in his life before. Even more tired than he had been that night at Campobello, when he was coming down with infantile paralysis.

He was so tired that he did not wear his leg braces when he went up to the Capitol to report to Congress on his trip. A few years ago he would not have dreamed of going without them. But this time he spoke sitting down.

Later he had gone up to Hyde Park for a few days, and he and Fala had driven up to

the little house he had had built for himself on the crest of a hill, with a magnificent view of the Hudson River valley.

After a few days back in the White House, they had come down to Warm Springs to his cottage, which was called the Little White House.

Already the rest had done him good. Everybody said he looked better. Out driving with Fala, with the top down, he had become a little tanned. The tired lines in his face were not so deep. And he was feeling better.

He was glad of that. For he had some big jobs ahead of him. And some big worries.

Although the war in Europe was almost over, the war with Japan must still be won, and it couldn't end until the Japanese surrendered.

That might mean that we'd have to take Tokyo. And to do it, we might lose a million men. The Japanese were tough fighters.

Stalin had promised that Russia would help as soon as the war in Europe was over. But would he keep that promise? He was already beginning to break some of the others he had made.

Well, perhaps the BIG SECRET the scientists were working on at Oak Ridge, Tennessee, and out in the state of Washington would produce what they hoped it would. With the atom bomb we might not need Stalin's help.

[169]

But there could be no way of knowing until they tried the bomb out, down in New Mexico. That would be sometime in July, they thought.

Yes, he had big worries. But he also had big plans—wonderful plans.

In a few days he would leave Warm Springs and go out to San Francisco. There the United Nations would be organized. The nations of the world were going to get together at last, to put a stop to wars.

The dream which Woodrow Wilson had had after World War I was finally going to come true. This time the nations, including the United States, had learned a lesson.

After San Francisco, he and his "Missis" were going to England, to return a visit King George and Queen Elizabeth had paid America in 1939. The President was looking forward to this trip.

Today was going to be the kind of day he loved, but couldn't often have. In the morning, a little work. After lunch a drive with Fala.

Late in the afternoon there was going to be a picnic. The newspapermen, the Warm Springs staff, and many Warm Springs friends would be there.

There would be Brunswick stew, a Southern dish made with chicken, which he loved. Graham Jackson, a Negro boy home on leave from the Coast Guard, would be on hand with his accordion. They'd get together a "barbershop" quartet and sing "Home on the Range."

And that evening he was going to a minstrel show, to be put on by the children who were patients at Warm Springs. They'd give him a greeting that always made him feel happy.

He heard the servants laughing in the kitchen. Lizzie MacDuffie, who had worked for the Roosevelts a long time, was still grinning when she came in with his breakfast tray, Fala scampering ahead of her.

"What were you all laughing about?" the President asked.

"Well, Mr. President," Lizzie explained, "we were talking about what we'd like to be if we could change into something else. Like a bird or an animal. And I said I'd like to be a little yellow canary flyin' around."

The President threw back his head and laughed—a great, booming laugh. Lizzie wasn't fat, but she was big.

"*You,* Lizzie—a little yellow canary!" he cried. "I love it! I love it!"

He stretched out his arms and flapped his hands up and down like wings. And they both laughed, until Lizzie had to take off her glasses and dry them on her apron.

Everybody in the house smiled. It was wonderful to hear the President laugh like that again.

The mail pouch from Washington was late that morning, and Bill Hassett, one of his secretaries, thought perhaps the President would like to let the work go until after lunch.

"No, Bill," the President said. "Let's do it now and get it over with."

They set up a card table in front of him, and he signed some letters and other papers, hanging them around the edge of the table for the ink to dry. He called this "hanging out his wash."

Congress had passed a bill, and it needed the President's signature before it would become a law.

"Here's where I make a law," he told Bill with a grin. And he signed his name with a flourish.

Bill left, and an artist who was painting his

[*172*]

"Here's where I make a law," he said, grinning

portrait arrived. He posed, sitting in his favorite chair by the fireplace.

It was almost one o'clock. A waiter came in and started to set the table for lunch.

Suddenly the President felt a sharp pain in his head. "I have a terrific headache," he said, looking surprised. And he put his hand up as if to wipe it away. Then he slumped forward in his chair. . . .

Before Mrs. Roosevelt left Washington by plane for Warm Springs that afternoon, she sent a message.

It went to Colonel James Roosevelt, U. S. Marine Corps; Lieutenant Commander Franklin D. Roosevelt, Jr., and Lieutenant John Roosevelt, U. S. Navy—all somewhere in the Pacific. It went also to Brigadier General Elliott Roosevelt, U. S. Army Air Corps, in England.

It did not have to be sent to Anna, for she was in Washington, where her little boy, Johnny, was in a hospital, seriously ill.

The message said:

"Father slept away. He would expect you to carry on and finish your jobs."

On the Burma Road in China an American soldier put his head down on his arms and cried when he heard the news.

"It can't be true!" he said. "It can't."

In St. Paul's Cathedral in London, Winston Churchill knelt and prayed.

And to the White House came a cablegram from the president of a little republic in South America. It said:

"There is not a single place on earth where this news will not cause disturbance and regret."

A procession led by a long black car filled with flowers stopped for a moment the next morning in front of Georgia Hall at Warm Springs. This was something the President always did when he was leaving to go back to Washington.

The patients were all out in front, in their wheel chairs, leaning on their crutches. But this time there was no cheering, no waving.

Graham Jackson was there, with his accordion. And the tears streamed down his cheeks as he softly played "Goin' Home."

All that night at dusty railroad crossings in the Carolinas and Virginia, crowds waited to see a train go by. Waited to catch a glimpse of a lighted car, filled with flowers, where four young men in uniform stood guard.

FRANKLIN D. ROOSEVELT

In Washington, thousands of people watched as a gun caisson, drawn by four black horses, moved slowly along Pennsylvania Avenue. They could see an American flag spread carefully over the coffin.

Arthur Godfrey tried to tell the American people about it, over the radio. But his voice broke. He couldn't go on.

At Hyde Park, it was bright and sunny in the rose garden behind the tall, dark hemlock hedge. That hedge along which a small boy used to ride a pony named Debbie, a long time ago.

Fala barked in sharp protest as rifles cracked in farewell salute across the banks of flowers laid on a flag-draped casket.

Later, a photographer wandering about the grounds took a picture. It appeared in many newspapers the next day.

It was a picture of a small black dog sitting on the front steps of a big house. Alone. Waiting.

About the Author

LORENA A. HICKOK was born in East Troy, Wisconsin. She went to Battle Creek High School in Michigan and then to the University of Minnesota. After college she wrote by-line stories for the *Minneapolis Tribune* for ten years. From 1928 to 1933, as an Associated Press writer, her stories were in newspapers all over the country, covering most of the important political events of that period. She knew President Roosevelt personally from 1928 until his death in 1945, first as a political writer and finally as a close friend of both Mr. and Mrs. Roosevelt. Miss Hickok now lives in Hyde Park, New York, right near the President's old home. She likes dogs, gardening, history, biography, and the Brooklyn Dodgers.

About the Artist

LEONARD VOSBURGH was born in Yonkers, New York, and grew up in Plainfield, New Jersey. He attended Pratt Institute and the Art Students League, and studied with such well-known artists as Harvey Dunn and Fritz Eichenberg. Before settling down in New York City, he visited all the states along the Eastern Seaboard. He is kept busy illustrating books for young people but also finds time to swim, collect antiques, and design and print linoleum blocks. Before starting the illustrations for THE STORY OF FRANKLIN D. ROOSEVELT, he visited Hyde Park and made careful, on-the-spot sketches of the scenes that figure in the story.

Signature Books

"Names That Made History"

ENID LaMONTE MEADOWCROFT, *Supervising Editor*

1 Born January 30, 1882,
at Hyde Park, New York

2 Graduates from Harvard University,

Marries Eleanor Roosevelt,
New York City, March 17, 1905

4 Appointed Assistant Secretary
of the Navy, 1913

9 War declared on Japan after the bomb
of Pearl Harbor on December 7, 194

Dies at Warm Springs, Georgia,
April 12, 1945

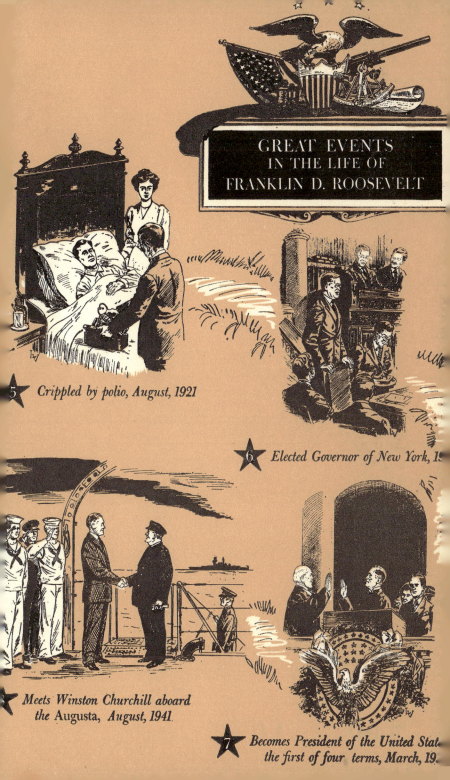

GREAT EVENTS
IN THE LIFE OF
FRANKLIN D. ROOSEVELT

5 *Crippled by polio, August, 1921*

6 *Elected Governor of New York, 1⁣9*

*Meets Winston Churchill aboard
the Augusta, August, 1941.*

7 *Becomes President of the United Stat⁣
the first of four terms, March, 19.*